MYSTIC
TAROT

PROJECTS EDITOR: Liz Wheeler
EDITOR: Ann Kay
ART DIRECTION: Zoë Maggs
DESIGN: John Bowles
ILLUSTRATION: Caroline Smith

This edition published by Barnes & Noble, Inc.
by arrangement with Carlton Books Limited.
2003 Barnes & Noble

ISBN 0-7607-4001-1
M 10 9 8 7 6 5 4 3 2 1

Printed and bound in China

MYSTIC
TAROT

MYSTIC MEG

WITH CARD ILLUSTRATION BY
CAROLINE SMITH

BARNES
&NOBLE
B O O K S
NEW YORK

CONTENTS

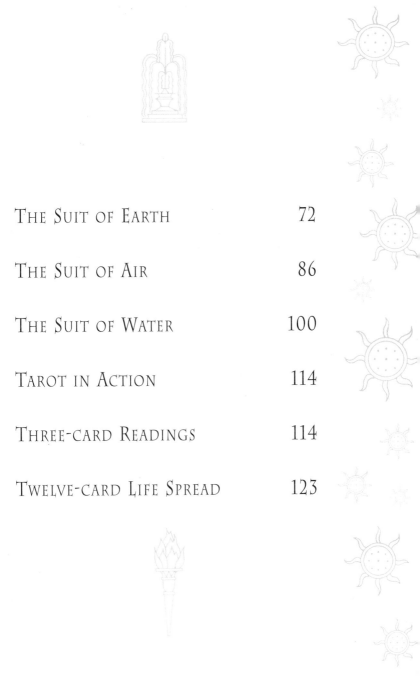

INTRODUCTION

My great-grandmother, who was a fortune-teller, taught me how to read the Tarot. From the first moment she unwrapped the pack of cards from the orange silk she kept them in, I have been fascinated by the Tarot. The images on even the most basic packs are truly powerful. And yet, for more than 20 years, I have been searching for the perfect set of cards. And then the Tarot itself gave me the answer. The most important card in my year-ahead reading was the High Priestess, telling me that I should work on a pack myself, with an artist whose illustrations and paintings are really inspiring. When I spoke to the painter Caroline Smith, she, too, knew that it was time to create a new Tarot pack.

These cards and this book are dedicated to all those who work with the Tarot, and all those who want to discover how to tell fortunes with the cards.

Mystic Meg

THE KEY TO
THE TAROT

The Tarot cards have much to tell you. To find out how they work, please shuffle the pack. Now divide the pack into three piles, and arrange them in a row. Take the top card from the centre pile. This is your guide card. Look at it for a moment and then put it where, from time to time, you can glance at it as you read these introductory pages.

THE 78 CARDS IN THE PACK

THE MAJOR ARCANA

The first 22 cards – each with its own name, and numbered 0 to 21 – are called the Major Arcana. The word "Arcana" means secrets, mysterious knowledge. The secrets are held in the images drawn on the cards. Although each one has a traditional interpretation, these images also stimulate the intuitive, creative sector of your mind.

If the guide card you've chosen is a Major Arcana card, then its initial meaning is that your life is going to be changed by outside events, major challenges, big opportunities.

THE MINOR ARCANA

The next 56 cards are called the Minor Arcana. This does not mean that they are less important; but they do work in a different way. The Minor Arcana is divided into four suits. Each suit has four court cards: Princess, Prince, Queen and King. If you have drawn one of these court cards, then the person you know, or will soon meet, who most resembles the figure on your card, holds the key to your present and your future.

Each suit also has ten cards, numbered one (or ace) to ten. If you have drawn one of these cards, then you are the prime mover, the one who can really influence events.

WHERE DID TAROT BEGIN?

The images on the Tarot, and the interest in predicting events through symbols, date back to Ancient Egypt and even older civilizations, right across the world. Tarot may have travelled to Europe from the Middle East at the time of the Crusades, in the 12th century. The earliest surviving cards are Italian, from the 15th century.

THE CARDS IN THIS PACK

I have known and admired the international artist and painter Caroline Smith for many years. And in these cards, she has created a beautiful and intriguing interpretation of the Tarot.

The Major Arcana cards in this pack use the traditional images in an inspiring way that is especially rich in meaning. And some of the names have been updated, to reflect the card's meaning more clearly.

The four suits of the Minor Arcana have many traditional names, but this pack links them with the four elements. So:
- the first suit is Fire (its older names include staves and wands)
- the second suit is Earth (also called pentacles and coins)
- the third suit is Air (also called swords and weapons)
- the fourth suit is Water (also called cups and vessels)

The Fire cards are represented by a torch of flames; the Earth cards by the tree; the Air cards by a bird in flight; and the Water cards by a fountain.

If your guide card is Fire, then be ready for action. If you have drawn an Earth card, look at the roots of your life, and at money and security. If you have drawn an Air card, it is time to let your mind fly free – ideas and communication matter now. If you have drawn a Water card, then your focus should be your emotions and all kinds of love and relationships.

LOVE, LIFE, LUCK AND COSMIC COUNSEL

For each card in the pack, I have given a reading under these four headings. Now turn to the page that holds a reading for your guide card. These mix traditional interpretation with the actual way in which the cards have worked in readings over many years.

When you have read my interpretation, look at your card again. You will find that your own intuition takes over and you will find extra, personal meanings.

CAN TAROT PREDICT THE FUTURE?

It looks like the new physics is proving what fortune-tellers have always believed – that time is just another dimension. So the future is already there, and is accessible to you. But the Tarot does not dictate the future. Instead it is an adviser, showing how your past, present and future all work together.

ARE SOME CARDS UNLUCKY?

No! But some do indicate a time of extra good fortune, a smooth path for love and relationships. Others reveal that you have challenges to accept and choices to make.

WHAT ABOUT CARDS COMING OUT OF THE PACK UPSIDE DOWN?

When a card is reversed, this does dilute the meaning a little, but does not change or darken the meaning.

HOW TO TELL FORTUNES

You must keep the cards safe and in good, psychic working order. So, when you are not using them, please keep them wrapped in a natural fabric, like silk or cotton. Before you start your reading, sit quietly for a few moments, so that your mind becomes calm and receptive. If you can, always lay out the cards on a wooden table. If you are new to the Tarot, deal yourself a card every day, so that you can familiarize yourself with the key points about each card.

When you are ready to tell your own, and other people's, fortunes, start by using a simple three-card deal (see Tarot in Action, page 114) to answer a question. Frequently asked questions are:

"Who is my perfect partner?"

"Does X love me?"

"Can this relationship be saved?"

"What kind of job is right for me?"

"Will I move house?"

"Will I ever win any money?"

Before the pack is shuffled, take out a "questioner" card. This should be the court card that most closely resembles the questioner – age, sex and character or zodiac signs are the keys here. Asking for someone's star sign can break the mood – if you don't know it, follow the character signals instead. First choose the suit, as follows:

FIRE CARDS for energetic, impatient people, and people with Aries, Leo and Sagittarius star signs.

EARTH CARDS for people who are serious about money, work and responsibility – and for people with Taurus, Virgo and Capricorn star signs.

12

AIR CARDS for those whose minds are their strongest muscle – and Gemini, Libra and Aquarius star signs.

 WATER CARDS for romantic, passionate and family-centred people – and those born under the signs of Cancer, Scorpio and Pisces.

If you are 25 or under, according to sex, use the Princess or Prince card. So a 22-year-old Gemini woman would be the Air Princess. If you are aged 26 or over, according to sex, use either the Queen or King card. So, for example, a 45-year-old Leo man would use the Fire King.

Put the questioner card close to the person you are reading for. Ask him or her to shuffle the cards and cut them into three piles (these don't need to be the same size). Now take the top card off each pile, one at a time.

Take the top card off the middle pile and use the love reading you'll find with that card in this book, and the Cosmic Counsel.
Take the top card from the left-hand pile (as you face it) and use the life reading given with that card.
The top card from the right-hand pile then takes the luck reading.

When you get used to reading the cards, there are more spreads at the back of this book (see page 114) for you to try. Because you are the one reading the cards, you will soon start picking up a wealth of information and insights from the images on the cards. That's the fun, the challenge and the magic of Tarot.

the BEGINNING

A journey begins. Childlike optimism, trust and innocence shine through. There is a guiding light of destiny, a loyal companion dog. But the crocodile is lurking – a reminder of danger for those who dare. This card represents fresh starts, excitement and, above all, a leap into the unknown. Linked to the rebel planet Uranus, it promises mystery, a dash of genius, adventure, and a brilliant opportunity to remake your life.

LOVE READING

Are you ready to risk everything for love? This card can show really strongly the beginning of a new relationship – one quite unlike any you have known before, because it is with someone who both looks and lives in a way outside your normal life. There is a strong link to travel, and to music. And an edge of danger that means you may never fully know, or trust, this partner. But the bonus is a kind of freedom and openness that lets you reach your full passion potential. You will learn to live, and love, for today rather than fretting about tomorrow. And stepping into a new world is a fantastic feeling.

If you are already in an established relationship, learning to let feelings flow rather than controlling them opens the gate to rich physical pleasure. You have a wild sexual imagination just waiting to be shared. This, plus a genuine effort to talk honestly and openly about love, can take a relationship along a path that's edged with excitement and enthusiasm. Taking time off to travel together, starting a joint business, even spending some time apart (with such sexy reunions!) are all possible new beginnings for a couple – especially if familiarity has diluted your passion. The moves you make now are very different, and very successful.

LIFE READING

The chance is coming to grab more excitement, more adventure. And the key is to let your own personality, opinions and talents show, instead of skulking behind someone else's. You have been scared to step out of line before. Now you have the courage to try new ways of working, of dressing, and even of relating to people around you. Your ideas may be a million miles from what people expect. But that is their strength, and the secret of your success. Work that links you to the world of dance, or children's entertainment, could be just right. And there is a surprising ally in a man who tells or writes jokes for a living, and is about to join your circle. Don't give up on a plan to live somewhere that others judge to be impossible. Routine is often cosy, but right now you need more. Destiny is leading you towards a road lined with identical trees.

You have gradually lost touch with your personal body rhythms and do need more structure to your patterns of eating, exercising and sleeping. Your body has so much to tell you – please listen, even if this means big changes.

LUCK READING

Good fortune for you goes hand in hand with children, so a child's birthday, or numbers chosen by someone much younger, can lead to winning luck. And there is such a strong luck-link to dogs, too. This card indicates that any house number, or phone number, that includes a zero is especially significant.

COSMIC COUNSEL

This is the one thought you must keep in your mind: "I have the courage to let go without losing. I am not afraid of the unknown."

1

MAGICIAN

the MAGICIAN

Appearances are not what they seem, says this card of illusion and creative energy. It shows a magician tapping into the boundless natural power of the universe, through the flash of lightning. Beneath him is a snake, ancient symbol of knowledge. This card is also connected to the mind planet Mercury, and shows that the imagination and creative ability needed to turn any life around is yours – now.

LOVE READING

Other people think they know you, and your love style, so well. But they are wrong. Because no one could guess how deeply passionate and uninhibited you really are. All you need is some help to shift your sensuous ideas from your brain to your body. This may come in the shape of someone with eyes like dark pools of mystery that hold your gaze despite yourself. Intense energy and a flamboyant dress style are further clues. This could be someone you already know. If not, you may meet in a place where lights flash and music plays – this person could have links to the showbiz world or a night-time job.

If you are in a relationship already, then it's a mistake to look outside it for new magic. All the passion potential you need is there, if you can find the way to channel it. As soon as you can, and certainly within the next month, you must conjure up some new, balanced love rules. Let reason rule romance and bring to an end a time when you've been a victim of emotional tricks. Strength and certainty are your gifts right now – use them wisely and well. Left unused, their special power could simply evaporate.

Drawing this card can often be a strong sign that your creative energy is about to be stretched – a special project may soak up most of it, leaving little for love. But if you are honest about this it could make your love-life more secure in the long run.

LIFE READING

The card of confidence, persuasive powers and ideas that inflame other people's imaginations – that's the Magician. Those around you are ready to be impressed, and it's your talent and skill that will do the trick. So, from today, believe in your plans and your hopes absolutely, especially any that link up in some way with making pictures or with helping people to look their best. Soon you will see those who matter following suit. There is much change in both your home and work environment. But it is the positive kind of change, which draws out hidden ambitions and gives you complete control over your cash situation.

Even if you have given up hope of having a calm, caring home of your own, you can in fact create this. But you must concentrate your energy on just one goal, rather than scattering it around.

Healthwise, overloading your body with rich food and drink late at night is out. A simple, balanced diet, with lots of fresh water, is in – plus taking time to be alone with your thoughts.

LUCK READING

Your best chance of winning prizes in life is when pictures, or words, are disguised in a certain way. A man who always uses the same catch-phrase is luck-linked for you, too, and when you travel the same distance in miles as your age, it brings back something – or someone – very special. This card's lucky number is 1.

COSMIC COUNSEL

Through challenging times, keep repeating this thought to yourself: "I am opening my mind and heart to good changes."

the HIGH PRIESTESS

All the mystery and intuition of the Moon merge with spiritual strength and psychic power – this is a card of discovery, both of self and others. So the High Priestess sits between two pillars – one dark, one light. This card shows you are ready to look deeper into life and love and face all sorts of secrets with warmth and compassion. There is also an undercurrent of touching tenderness, and the ability to read other people's minds.

LOVE READING

Whether you are in a relationship or still looking for love, this card gives you special intuition to see past false faces and false feelings to the true desires beneath. And this can draw new, exciting lovers to you, or reawaken the spark that's dulled between a current couple.

Someone with a calm, pale face, who is often to be found surrounded by books, may play a really vital role in your emotional future. Yes, even if this person has a far-from-perfect passion history, love will last this time around. So don't let outside pressures, or whispers, put off your small, quiet inner voice.

If you are in a relationship already, then make the most of your psychic powers to place warm, loving feelings in a certain special mind. But beware – this will only work if you are sincere.

LIFE READING

Stop doubting and start deciding – this is the card of trusting your own instincts instead of being confused by other people's words. And it shows that you have been swamped with so much advice, from so many sources, that you've ended up stuck to the spot. Now it's time to make the move that will take you closer to helping people with either your hands or your voice. Special links are strongly indicated between you and the world of healing.

Learning a new skill or gaining a new qualification are good moves too – please don't let a difficult circumstance, or a lot of competition, put you off. This card shows you have the ability and the special something needed to succeed where others fail. When it comes to cash questions, gentle probing achieves a far better result than impatient arguments.

At home, your longing to protect people could have the opposite effect and push them away. Please remember that the true test of love is learning to let go. And if it is something in your own life that spills over into others, the time is right to face it.

While you wait for the chance to implement major home changes, try some simple ideas to make the most of what you have now. A lot of the stress you feel comes from your own expectations – and so you can easily control it.

Anxiety about health matters, especially linked to children, pushes a positive outcome further away. Please try to find a way of letting worries and doubts slide away every night before you go to sleep.

LUCK READING

When a baby's name, or face, is entered in a local competition – perhaps in secret – it can lead to national prizes. A woman who works in the property business, and the number 2, are also luck-bringers.

COSMIC COUNSEL

Repeat this message to yourself, every day: "There is no end to the talents I have, and I must not waste a single one of them."

the EMPRESS

With the sceptre in one hand and wheat in the other, the Empress represents the rule of nature and the natural world. This is a wonderfully positive sign of nurturing both physical and emotional needs, and also a strong symbol of fertility. Wearing the emblem of love planet Venus, the woman on this card promises harmony at work and at home – marriage, security and warmth.

LOVE READING

If you have lost confidence in your personal power to attract, and keep, love, then this can change now. For as soon as you start to believe in your right to respect, and to romance, then the door will be opened on a treasure house of emotional and physical pleasures. A meeting in a place where food is sold, or where people are eating, is the one to awaken sudden, yet sure, emotions. And the perfect partner for you is someone dark, expensively dressed, and with a mix of tenderness and wild abandon that promises a lifetime of excitement. And a lifetime it will be, if that is what you want. For whatever the problems in your past, drawing this card shows that you are now ready to give, and receive, the kind of commitment that just goes on getting stronger. Love will feed your emotions and satisfy your body.

If you are already in a relationship, then look again at your pattern of everyday loving. Practical problems and day-to-day events have pushed passion to the bottom of your priority list. So your wild side, your more dangerous desires and fantasies, have been tamed too much. Please try to find a better balance.

And remember – you can care for someone without having to own them. Passion does not include possession.

LIFE READING

This is a card of wealth and generosity, and the time of calm prosperity that it promises pushes out past problems and bad memories. There is possible income that is linked to a woman who is well-built, older than you, a mother, and wears jewellery made of three different kinds of gold. But you must wait for her to come to you, please don't try to rush the process! And put a cash agreement on hold until you know more about it.

You have hidden talents linked to designing or making something for children, perhaps clothes or toys. And helping someone older to solve a property puzzle has a financial spin-off for you, too.

This card connects you to the countryside, and a move in that direction is likely. But remember that no amount of travelling can solve a problem that's at the centre of your life. Only you can do that, by standing still and facing facts. Please believe that this is the symbol of strong family happiness, however unlikely this seems to you right now.

Life as other people's go-between saps your strength. Replace it with personal care – long, slow massages of the back or feet, and some scented oil in a warm bath. And keep food simple, plain, and low key in salt and spice.

LUCK READING

Cards coloured like jewels, learning words in a new language and the number 3 are all ringed with luck for you.

COSMIC COUNSEL

Keep these special words safe in your heart: "I am filled with love and beauty that I am privileged to share with the world."

the EMPEROR

The rather stern-looking Emperor on this card holds an orb and sceptre, symbols of both royalty and responsibility. This is a card of leadership, power and strength, signified by the throne that the Emperor is sitting on. The added connection of star sign Aries underlines the elements of energy and courage, but also suggests tenderness under the toughness. Great to have on your side, yet a challenge card, too.

LOVE READING

Someone who seems so in control may be secretly seething with love feelings for you – and you will meet first at a sporting or other outdoor event. How will you recognize this potential partner? It will be someone in a position of authority, with a face full of character and a smile that is rarely seen but still lights up the room. A royal-linked name is a further clue, but the real proof is provided when hands touch, and an electric current of physical attraction starts to spark. This will be a relationship of challenges, and communication channels must be kept open at all costs. And if you can't accept a partner who must always be in charge, think carefully before you start to commit your heart.

If you are already locked in love, drawing this card indicates that passion may be taking second place to power games. Clever words and cold criticism are no substitute for simple physical warmth. And a partner who seems cool about a new commitment, perhaps to marriage, children or a house move, is covering secret insecurity. When you say yes, and show your own optimism, the answer you want will follow, as you encourage your partner.

LIFE READING

Recent slow-downs in your working world are set to end when an announcement of a new job, or a good change in your present one, shows just how well you really are regarded. And there is a special ally already in your circle, or about to enter it. This is a man with a powerful body and a loud, confident voice, who scares many people. If you start to treat him as an equal, however, your reward will be his friendship and trust forever.

This card strongly advises you to lock strong emotions in your heart and apply cool logic to problems instead. You can get the cooperation you need from a family, but through negotiation, not displays of power or temper. Look again at the rules, or plans, that you expect others to follow. If they aim too high, don't be too proud to think again. You will lose nothing; gain so much. A man in a colourful jacket can help with a legal matter.

It is important to trust your cool judgement when someone you care about asks for financial help, but won't explain what the money is for. You must find a different way to help him or her.

Cool your inner temperature with plenty of plain water and cleansing fruit teas. And burn off that pent-up energy, which could so easily explode into temper, with competitive sport.

LUCK READING

Look again at those mind-stretching puzzles you've been afraid to try before. You have the brain power to do brilliantly! Luck is also linking you with travel, your father's family and a legacy. And there's a cash bonus when your face appears in a surprising place. This card highlights number 4 as a luck-maker for you.

COSMIC COUNSEL

Say this each night before you sleep: "I am in charge of my own life. I have the power to make my hopes come true."

the HIGH PRIEST

Followers kneel at the feet of the High Priest to hear his words of wisdom, and also in the picture are the two crossed keys, representing knowledge and understanding. This is the card of guidance and teaching, but also of personal conscience. It suggests you can get advice from many sources, but only you can apply it to your own life. Linked to Taurus, it reminds you of the value of loyalty and of being trustworthy, even when others seem not to be.

LOVE READING

Do you feel that love has let you down, that it has never quite lived up to your expectations? And does this colour every relationship, old and new, in your life? Well, drawing this card shows that this situation is set to change. First, it points to a perfect partner for you as someone quite a bit older, who may wear a moon-shaped symbol. You will meet this person when you approach a group you want to join, or ask for some special medical or legal advice.

This time around, you will have the strength to ask for the love role that you know you need right from the very start. For in all relationships, even in ones that are long-established, you do need to be in charge some of the time. It's always important that a partner really understands this. And outside help may be needed to help free ideas that have rusted up with everyday routine. Only you hold the key to your own inner knowledge and peace. Please don't be afraid to use it – and soon.

LIFE READING

There are two very different work success routes showing up for you. One takes you straight to the centre of a special group or company, with a way of working that has always attracted you, even though the financial gain may be less.

The other leads you towards training in a career that heals damaged bodies – or spirits. Whichever way you choose, it will not be an overnight change, but a very gradual process. And you must be sure that profit does not take priority over keeping your conscience clear.

There are strong signs that you will be travelling back towards a town or country where your family once lived, and this can answer so many questions, both about your past and your future. At home, try to ignore small family niggles and keep your eyes and mind on the long-term future. Soon a family will need to pool strength to tackle big changes. Save your energy for that.

Get up off that sofa and walk in the open air as much as you can. You will help your health and refresh your mind. Do make sure that you take a careful approach to eating. An expert opinion – perhaps from an outside source – may be the final push you need to make a medical decision, or to help someone close to make certain health choices.

LUCK READING

Someone who hides a smart, funny mind behind a so-serious face can bring prizes your way, especially in a contest you enter together. Crosses in different colours, a name famous for giving advice, and the number 5 are all layered with special luck, too.

COSMIC COUNSEL

Repeat to yourself, every day and every night: "I am open to help and advice – I am looking forward now, and not back."

25

the LOVERS

The card of romantic choices, passion and temptation. The image shows two lovers who are close but, in the gap between them, is the snake of temptation, coiled around the tree. The face looking down represents the power of love, but it is linked with the Gemini star sign, so there are two ways to use this love – wisely or recklessly. This is both an intriguing and exciting card.

LOVE READING

You will soon be facing a love decision because this card holds two very different partners for you. One person is kind and loving, and offers you nourishment and security in both heart and home. This person is already close to you and you have only to reach out. But there is still a small gap between you. And that is leaving room for a second person to snake into your life.

This second partner seems to have a direct link to your passion dreams and the relationship would be propelled by the most powerful physical attraction. This does not mean love would not work, but it would demand a great deal from you. You would need to be very independent and emotionally secure to deal with this partner. Partly because he, or she, will always attract other people. And partly because of the rather glamorous or even dangerous way this person makes a living. So you do need to think carefully about this option.

With your first choice, you would need extra effort to make your bodies communicate as richly as your hearts. But you have drawn this card, and so you certainly do have lots of passion potential – although so far you have not used it to the full in your love relationships.

If you are already settled in a relationship, you do need to reach out and close that gap. And, for your own love happiness, it is important that you make clear, sincere choices. Trying to run two relationships could lead to losing both of them.

LIFE READING

Both your working life and your home-life will involve choices, too. The whole situation at home could change and you may find yourself swapping roles with a partner, or starting up a home-linked business. You have twin talents here – one is linked to pets, and the other has a direct link to love. You could have some kind of involvement with the business side of a marriage bureau. A cash gift from a married couple, who also work together, will help you with plans to make your home-life exactly what you want it to be.

However, your family loyalties are squeezed when two people ask you to take sides – please avoid this.

You need to improve the quality of your sleep. Tell yourself that tomorrow is time enough to deal with the questions on your mind and give yourself permission to sleep sweetly.

LUCK READING

Your best chance of winning prizes is to take part in a contest that takes love as its theme. And a country that lovers made famous is going to play a lucky part in your life. This card also circles number 6 as a luck-bringer. It could soon appear on a wedding invitation.

COSMIC COUNSEL

Put this thought in your mind: "I have the right and the power to make my own choices, and I know these choices will be so good."

7

CHARIOT

the CHARIOT

Movement, activity, progress and travel are the main themes of this challenging card. There could be a battle to win, too – for that special partner or position. The Chariot is pulled by two winged horses. These are symbols of power that fly high above the ordinary, but they also face in different directions, so you need to take charge. Warrior planet Mars promises victory in love and life and total honesty between hearts.

LOVE READING

After so long stuck in stalemate, love is on the move again in your life. If you are still seeking a loving partner, then someone who drives a lot as part of their job, or works for a travel-linked company, may be your fate mate. And you could well meet for the first time where a journey begins. There may be competition for this person's love, either from past or present partners. But you have the strength to win, never doubt that.

Drawing this card can be a warning against selfish behaviour within a relationship – such as one partner chasing their own dreams and desires without consulting, or including, the other. And if you are already locked in a happy love-bond, then this card is saying, quite strongly, that it needs a rethink. You do need – and you deserve – more. And yes, a partner will be ready to give it, this time around.

With your physical and emotional energy at an all-time high for the next four weeks, this is the time to start steering love in a direction that you choose, rather than simply accepting any old route. Showing that you have needs will leave you more loved, not less. And a journey that a couple make together ends a time of doubt and ensures that a rival is no longer a problem.

LIFE READING

You have two major voyages of discovery to make. The first takes you towards a kind of job success that is linked to travel, or perhaps living abroad. But this will be a wasted excursion unless you also make a more demanding inner journey, this time from uncertainty to confidence, in your own skills and your own future. There is a special role in this development for anything to do with driving, from taking lessons to motor racing. And a house (or other building) near a busy road plays a part.

Your home-life is looking secure again after a time of upsets, as a cloud cast by an official complaint or interference clears. But this card urges complete honesty where cash, and family, are concerned. If you have gone wrong somewhere, you must admit it – don't try to hide it. And beware of dressing up difficult facts to spare someone else's feelings. Your motives may be for the best, but they are mistaken.

The first move towards ending a feud must come from you. It may not feel fair, but it's the only way forward. Be generous and brave enough to make it, and soon.

Living life in a hurry can hurt your health. Do eat plenty of fruit and vegetables. And walk whenever you get the chance.

LUCK READING

Wins spin your way when you link up with someone who works, or lives, in several different countries. Cars are yours to win, and the number 7 is lucky too, especially printed inside a circle.

COSMIC COUNSEL

Clear your mind of all thoughts except this one: "I can achieve inner peace, and this will bring great success to my outer life."

JUSTICE

With the sword of justice in one hand and the scales of equality in the other, this card is certainly not to be taken lightly! It represents balance, fairness, decisions and legal affairs, and is also a strong symbol of second chances in love. Allied with fair-minded star sign Libra, Justice promises fair shares for all, but the action may be delayed while all possibilities are weighed – to get the best possible result.

LOVE READING

If passion favours one partner in a relationship too much, then drawing this card means balance will soon be restored. But there is a cost: both sides must be ruthlessly honest about what they want, and why. And decide to make major decisions together, rather than one partner setting off on a path while the other trails resentfully behind. Soon you will find yourself in a really mutually satisfying relationship.

If you are still looking for love, then someone with close links to the law, who may wear a uniform, could be very important. For those with an unhappy passion past, ending in divorce or separation, you could not have a stronger sign that, yes, you will marry again. And this time it will be a match of equals. This card also urges you to consider someone who already has children, and may already be in your circle.

Although love often feels like a trial to you, it need not be. Tension comes from seeing a relationship as a test you have to pass, rather than a loving, sharing team. Self-criticism makes you too tough on yourself – relax into romance and all will go well.

If you are at a love crossroads, and wondering which way to choose, then this card reminds you that clean breaks help best. But you must get the right legal advice you need. And avoid any situation that stains your conscience.

LIFE READING

Work will start to go well again when you pursue your own ambition, instead of adopting someone else's goal. You have the power, and the ability, to make such strong and good decisions. Job luck is linked to writing, inventions and the world of law.

Balance will soon be back in your home-life, as a situation that drains away too much of your time and energy is set to change. Stop struggling to hold a couple, or a team, together. It's time for a new start, deep down you do know that. Let them make their own choices.

Keep cash and family arrangements as simple as possible. There is so much in your life that is excess baggage and can be booted out. Then feel how much richer yet lighter you are. You'll be back in control.

Talking through health or happiness problems can throw up such an unexpected yet obvious answer. If you can't find someone you trust enough, perhaps a sensitive stranger is the answer. Artificial boosts like fizzy drinks, tea, coffee and cigarettes mask your real energy levels. Cut back and see truly positive results.

LUCK READING

Identifying missing parts of words or pictures puts you on a prize list. Number 8 is lucky – as is a trip linked to a famous name from the past and a talent for recognizing antiques.

COSMIC COUNSEL

Hold these words close to your heart: "The best decisions are the ones that I make for myself – I truly believe in my own strength."

9 ♍ ♍

the HERMIT

Separated from the outside world by a protective shell, the Hermit illustrated on this card still holds a brilliant star that illuminates the way ahead, and is surrounded by the wisdom of the zodiac. So space and time away from everyday concerns can be the key to self-knowledge and self-confidence. Linked to Virgo, and the search for information, this card is a guiding light – a promise of brighter times.

LOVE READING

If you are looking for love, then someone who you first read about in a local paper or newsletter could be the right one. Yes, even if this person has links to a world that seems so strange and new to you. Perhaps this involves alternative medicine or other therapies. The attraction will be so very real and true – and will grow into a relationship that, at last, answers your emotional as well as physical needs.

A vague feeling that passion has not quite reached its full potential for you needs further thought, and then action. For the only person who can make this situation change is you. It seems you have shut yourself off from feelings you see as risky, and built a high wall of humour, or smart talk, to protect your tender heart.

But love will not flourish when only pleasure is shared and problems are hidden. You need quiet time alone, as soon as you can, to think through what you really want from love. Put this hope first in your heart, then it can start to happen. And however far a relationship has gone down the wrong road, it can be reversed. Take a very tactful approach when you ask for changes.

LIFE READING

A work dream can become so much more, but first you must break away from a situation that has run its course. Only by doing this can you try out some new, very different ideas, or make plans for your own progress. Your judgement is clouded while others' demands and dramas surround you. But although you do have the inner strength to succeed in all you do, this will not happen without the right foundation of physical and mental fitness. So step back from those habits that are starting to harm your health or your happiness.

Meetings with older – or maybe just wiser – people are indicated. They will share information and experience that you can use in your own special way.

A time you have found difficult at home is drawing to a close. If you have felt isolated, this will end with a house move, or a major rethink of where you live now. This will include getting the special space you know you need to get a creative plan moving.

Someone far away from your family need not be gone forever. An unusual way of getting in touch, perhaps through flowers or food, is the key to making a family whole again. To keep it that way, be honest about your troubles as well as your triumphs.

Get back in touch with your body through simple stretches and calming foods. Take a few minutes each morning to settle your thoughts. And meditation would be just right for you.

LUCK READING

Links with someone who lives alone are really lucky for you, plus identifying mystery faces or places. Number 9 is a fortune-finder.

COSMIC COUNSEL

The Hermit's watchword to you is this: "I care for myself as much as for others – now I can reach out to life and make my mark."

33

the WHEEL OF FORTUNE

The circle of life, and of fate, spins on this card of changes. Below the wheel lurks the serpent of deep, dark times. Above it is the sphinx of airy freedom and insight. This reminds us that fortune can turn either way, but both have much to teach us. Jupiter, planet of golden luck, is strongly linked to this card, too.

LOVE READING

The wheel of fortune is turning now, and moving you away from the people and the situations that have been hurting your heart. And, tempting though it is to cling on to familiar feelings and faces, even ones that are bad for you, the strongest message of this card is one of letting go, and looking forward.

You should also be leaving past love mistakes behind and trying out a new love-style. This is one that adds self-respect to an element of mystery, and stops you rushing into requests for commitment before either side is ready. If you are in a relationship, you will feel the effects of this confidence swing in two ways. First, you can accept a partner's need for separate time, or space, without panicking. Second, you will find the perfect blend of fiery physical loving and affectionate romance to make love feel so fresh.

If you are looking for love, someone bursting with energy, with dark hair and pale eyes, could be your perfect partner. This is someone who spins through a high-speed life with an image that constantly changes. And you could meet somewhere with a circular dance-floor or stage. This time love will be all you hope for – if you remember past problems and learn from them.

LIFE READING

Change is natural, sometimes unstoppable – so it is good to deal with it. Welcoming it puts you in a stronger position. For at last difficult times are being left behind as you spin in a new direction, towards new opportunities. Please, open your mind, and your heart, to change. The biggest mistake you can make is to cling too tightly to old, safe ideas – you will miss exciting new ones.

At work, acknowledge your faults as well as your good points, and build on both of them. Drawing this card can indicate that you are pushing yourself in the wrong direction, going against the flow of fate instead of with it. Take that step towards retraining, or reapplying, for a dream job. This time it will work.

Time and energy that you gave freely in the past pays off in the present, as a gift of cash or gold. And it will help you to make a commitment that seems far out of reach. Family history is about to repeat itself, in all the right ways. A house with a wheel-shaped gate or window is the key.

Unsatisfactory health patterns are ending, and a new, fitter you can become a reality. And this card also reveals a return visit to a health location, for a very welcome reason.

LUCK READING

A building with a revolving door plays a large part in your luck profile, along with a wheel filled with numbers and letters. And stand by for a magic meeting when you travel to a town built round a circular lake. Fortune's figure for this card is number 10.

COSMIC COUNSEL

Keep this thought in your mind today: "I am ready to leave the past and look to the future. I will say yes to life's challenges."

STRENGTH

Emotional courage, physical strength and positive action link up like the garland of flowers on this card's powerful yet gentle image. A beautiful woman effortlessly controls a fierce lion, but through calm self-confidence, not force or fear. And this courage is echoed in links with fearless star sign Leo. Tenderness and toughness fuse and two apparent opposites make an unbeatable problem-solving team.

LOVE READING

This card can show that passion has been draining away in a drawn-out quarrel – fear of losing face makes both sides afraid to give in. But when two people decide, together, to focus on the strengths of love rather than its weaknesses, feelings are ready and waiting to be rediscovered. This time, honest feelings like trust and loyalty will triumph, and jealousy and revenge be pushed out. And yes, a promise will be renewed.

Before you can reach this point, however, you may need to stand outside a relationship for a while and take the time you need to calm inner turmoil. Drawing this symbol is a really strong suggestion that a man needs to listen to a woman's advice, or tune in more to his own feminine side. And, if you are still seeking a lifetime love, then learning to feel more confident and content in your own company could be the key to a successful relationship.

The perfect fate mate for you could work closely with animals, or in a job connected to fitness. And this time, passion will leave your mind and your heart as satisfied as the rest of your body. You will be amazed at the new levels of spiritual and physical loving that open to you. Keep your body in sexy shape with some gentle exercise – you'll soon be glad you did.

LIFE READING

You are moving into a time when you will feel much stronger and in control. So you can talk calmly and openly about conflict rather than stewing in secret. This leads to new success at work, and a second chance at a test or meeting that didn't go well last time. It's never too late to try again, especially if your heart whispers that a work path is actually someone else's idea.

You can discover the trick of channelling powerful feelings like anger or jealousy into creative projects, and relax in the knowledge that you are more than a match for a difficult group of people you are asked to lead.

At home, secret frustration is withering a family's happiness – please speak out, even if it means asking for more than you usually do. Resist promises of easy money; it's your time to try saving, not spending.

Help your health by cutting time-wasters – personal and professional – out of your life. You have every right to your own time, your own ideas. Build stamina with a daily walk and make sure you eat breakfast every day.

LUCK READING

Number 11 is this card's key figure – for you, it could mean double money-luck from a question linked to foreign wildlife. A fairground or amusement arcade could find you fortune, especially in a contest linked to strength. Your colours are warm brown and honey yellow – wear them for good luck.

COSMIC COUNSEL

Tell yourself every day: "My own voice is the one I hear – and I now have the courage to be whatever, and whoever, I want."

37

12 ♆ ▽

SELF-
SACRIFICE

It looks scary, but once you have taken the plunge you never want to go back – this is a strong symbol of losing something familiar in order to gain richer understanding and a new start. The figure suspended from the rope looks calm, almost detached, supported by belief in the future. The link-planet Neptune looks for answers in dreams. The rune alphabet on the pillars tells of secret knowledge that will soon come to you if you open your mind.

LOVE READING

Emotional affairs are heading for a complete change-around. This may mean a sudden new rush of romance and love into a relationship already tossed and tested on stormy emotional seas. After a time of such frustrating non-commitment, things are moving again, and it's all going your way. But you still need to be brave, and bold – few changes come without a struggle, even pleasant ones. It's not easy to let go of old love habits, even if they are not working well now.

You should back away from someone else's feelings and give a relationship some breathing space. You are at a crossroads, but both ways lead into the light.

If you are still searching for love right now, you are most likely to meet your partner when you are not really looking. Someone with links to air travel or healing, and who uses another language every working day, could be the right one for you. There may be an element of waiting involved – perhaps this person is not free straight away. But the patience and tolerance you are learning will last for the rest of your lifetime. And you will see that outward wealth is no match at all for inner peace.

As you learn that love can call on you to give things up and to make changes on behalf of other people, you will at last fit the missing pieces to the puzzle of your heart.

LIFE READING

The signs are strong that you have, until now, settled for work that does not stretch or fulfil your mental strengths. Or perhaps you have accepted a lifestyle that is really too conventional for you. Well, change is coming, but it will be gradual.

You are in the process of maturing mentally and may find satisfaction in striking out on your own in the world of work. Choose any field linked to photography, film or television.

At home, a time of feeling the odd one out, or of waiting for someone else to change, is ending now. You must learn to accept other people's chosen paths with less personal anxiety.

Physically, you have denied yourself enough rest and isolation. Let mind and body drift in a candlelit bath. Play music with no words. Lighten your spirits by surrounding yourself with light and air, and with cool greens and blues.

LUCK READING

Any exchange in which no money swaps hands will hold hidden luck for you, along with the number 12, especially within a time schedule. A broken household object brings a cash bonus, but beware of throwing out a prize ticket – this card indicates a holiday win that is almost overlooked.

COSMIC COUNSEL

Write down your dreams every day and repeat these words to yourself: "I face the unknown and I am not afraid any more."

CHANGING

Look at the tree of life on this card – half in winter, half in summer; half sunshine, half shade. It reminds us of both the inevitability and the rhythmic nature of change – above all, that change is a natural thing. Symbol of transformation, fertility and (with links to star sign Scorpio) sexuality, this card shows that, by accepting the loss of old love, old links and old ideas, life opens to great new gains.

LOVE READING

Sometimes, this card highlights what you fear losing in a relationship – even if you know that a coming change is inevitable, you struggle against it. But even the kind of upheaval that you most dread need not spell disaster. Because your reaction suggests that you are suppressing your feelings and must let yourself speak out, and reach out, very soon. Then love can shift into a new dimension.

Yes, this card of sudden change may also show an earthquake shaking what seems like a rock-solid relationship. This tremor may be an outside rival, a change in one partner's expectations or demands, or even an acceptance that letting go and moving on is your only choice now. But every ending, however difficult, contains the seeds of a new beginning. And you must believe that your love-life is becoming much, much stronger.

If you are still on a love-search at the moment, someone who wears bright, jewel-like colours and works in gardening, crime-solving or medicine, could be the one for you. And this relationship will be profoundly passionate, and healing.

LIFE READING

There is rapid progress ahead in your home-life. Where a family has been broken up, or living arrangements disrupted, there will be a fast, fresh start. And the more enthusiastically you welcome the sudden changes facing you, the better the outcome will be.

Financially, there may be a sweeping loss. But it will lead to a regular rise in income that more than makes up for it. This is a good time, however, to review your saving and spending plans and tip the balance more towards saving.

An object or person from your family's past is going to give you a firm clue as to which direction your working path should take next. Chances are that there is an idea sprouting deep in your heart that just needs some light, and encouragement, to grow fast.

If you have been feeling bogged down by life lately, then free yourself by removing clutter from your living and working space. Only display those objects and pictures that you really like, and pack away everything else. And make every effort to apply the same kind of sweep-clean strategy to your health. Drink more plain water, bottled or filtered, and clean up your diet by switching from processed to fresh food.

LUCK READING

Red and black, seen in strong patterns together, are luck indicators for you. So is the number 13, especially on a door or as part of a date of birth. And walking over a floor with a geometric design takes you much closer to a family truth. Sealed containers and valuable gifts in small boxes are both going to lead you towards very special and unique friendships.

COSMIC COUNSEL

Relax your mind, and then repeat to yourself: "All that has gone before, including my mistakes, is preparation for my new life tomorrow. And this new life will be the right one for me."

14

TEMPERANCE

This is a soothing symbol of balance, healing and beautiful music, which may be made by either instruments or bodies. The winged figure on the card pours the waters of truth in exactly the right proportions, to help you know much more about your inner self, and the outside world. There is a powerful flow of energy renewing itself, which is reflected in ties with Sagittarius, star sign of youth and knowledge.

LOVE READING

You must either introduce proper balance into your love-life, or let someone else do it for you. The signs are that a present relationship is lop-sided – either too physical, or led too much by one partner. Ask yourself why you are afraid to look closer at the reasons for this. Just because an arrangement has worked in the past, does not make it right for the future.

You may need to look outside the relationship to find what you need – in the form of friendship, fun, a very different kind of conversation. If you feed the benefits of this back into your love-bond, it will not suffer. In fact, when you give a partnership more room to breathe, it can often make love healthier. And this card's links with child-like, easy-going Sagittarius show that a lighter approach could be the best way out of some heavy problems.

This card may signal a long, straight talk that resolves heartache and helps one partner come to terms with a change in a joint lifestyle. Or it can predict marriage.

If you are looking for love, then be ready for an unusual, free-and-easy romance with a person who refuses to play conventional love roles. Look for a calm face and kind voice that speaks straight to your heart. Some kind of musical talent is also indicated. You will meet in a place where water flows and blue clothes are worn.

LIFE READING

Tact and treading carefully are your two keynotes at work. You have some really great ideas but do need help to make them happen. And this will come when you step back, lower your stress levels and wait for interest to be expressed. Good paths pointed to by this card include health foods, counselling and alternative therapies.

Try to stay semi-detached from others' arguments – use quiet, deep-breathing techniques to keep cool when tempers start to flare. Those who really matter will notice so much more than you think.

But remember – letting cash, or the search for it, push its way into your mind must at the same time push some other things out. Healthy relationships and inner harmony are worth more than money. Sort out these aspects of your life, and the cash will sort itself out. You could find a new home near a water's edge, or close to a place where two very different landscapes meet. A couple who have only just met, or have just got together again, will soon have some baby news.

LUCK READING

A prize centres on a voyage or party linked to boats. And you could be a winner with the number 14. Plus your timing brings a surprise bonus when something delivered early brings a ticket-shaped thank-you. Second time around yields brilliant test results.

COSMIC COUNSEL

Before any major task in life, repeat these words to yourself: "I make the most of my talents, and make allowances for my faults."

43

15 ♑ ♒

TEMPTATION

TEMPTATION

Sexual desire, money and power-lust – the strongest of instincts lie at this card's roots. And the chained figures of a man and a woman show how hard it can be to break free. This card represents the facing of a difficult truth, a key choice that could easily tempt you in the wrong direction. But cool-headed Capricorn is also in the mix to offer self-control and the determination to find a better way of living.

LOVE READING

Despite this card's fearsome face, there is a positive message coming through. In a relationship, a period of darkness is now going to let in some light, and there is a promise of loving reconciliation between two powerfully opposed characters, or perhaps families.

There is a strong indication of fertility here, too, especially if a couple have been trying for a child without success. And a relationship is about to become more practical, perhaps through starting a home together, or merging home and work jointly.

This card also indicates sudden, unexpected physical attraction. Yes, this can be between established partners, who suddenly find new ways of showing passion, providing pleasure and diving deeper into exploring love instead of staying safely on the surface. But this desire can be an outside threat that overwhelms one partner, too, and could put a relationship in peril without some honest talking.

If your heart is free at the moment, this card signals an exciting new sexual encounter, one that could awaken someone physically for the first time. Trust your instincts when you meet someone truly hypnotic and irresistible. The danger lies in letting your heart rule your head and in missing the signs of desire used as a controlling force, rather than a shared pleasure.

LIFE READING

Yes, it's tempting to think about using information at work to get back at an old enemy. But resisting this is what will get you noticed, and could lead to the promotion or pat on the back that is indicated by this card. The signs are that you will feel torn between your own ambition and someone else's – beware of success clouding your conscience and leading to less-than-honest use of others' ideas.

Your home-life will be influenced by an older, wealthier person – but remember that a long-term loan or other hand-out may have more strings attached than you really want. You do have the strength to reach a goal alone – don't be tempted to compromise.

Part of a family that's been in shadow comes into the light again. This may lead to difficult times, but you will learn so much about living and loving. Accepting demanding responsibilities is one choice – trying to break free is another. You can defeat a habit that's become almost an obsession – perhaps linked to food, drink or exercise. And doing so will help your health all round.

LUCK READING

Specialist knowledge of an unusual subject sets you on a winning streak. And number 15 and a carved wooden figure of a child are linked, too, in lucky ways. Fortune flies from a phone call.

COSMIC COUNSEL

When temptation strikes, remember this message: "I can have whatever I want, but am I prepared to pay the very high price?"

the TOWER

Lightning flashes, day turns to night, cracks appear – so it's no surprise that this card heralds huge and often unexpected change. But, unlike the figures falling or leaping to escape their fate, you have time to prepare. And the energy of planet Mars, plus the totally transforming element of fire, gives you the power you need to turn upheaval to inspiration, changes to challenges that can make you strong.

LOVE READING

It looks as if a relationship needs kick-starting into life again – or even picking apart and getting right back to basics. You may secretly sense what is wrong and be scared of looking further. Now circumstances force your hand and make change necessary.

Very often, drawing this card indicates coming events that completely change the focus of a love affair, perhaps switching the power balance and bringing back the kind of raw energy and reckless passion that has been seeping away. The key to this can be an air-clearing row that taps into Mars' anger as well as action. After a long time in the wilderness, two people speak honestly, without tears or tantrums, and turn what could be such a destructive influence into a positive driving force. Love will never be the same again, but will start afresh on better, braver foundations – if you are resolute.

For those in search of love, this card highlights someone with a thrilling hobby or physically dangerous job as prime partner material. However wrong this person seems for you at first, your emotions will feel so right. And this feeling is what you should follow. Instant dislike will turn to desire and the bond will be stimulating and sensual, and never taken for granted.

LIFE READING

An established way of life is suddenly in upheaval – changes in where you live, how and where you work and who is central to your happiness, are all tied up in the Tower card.

In your working world, authority could break down, with control handed to an unexpected, and possibly unwelcome, pair of hands. But if you show you can adapt to change quickly, you will soon turn this strain to success – on your terms.

Be prepared for sudden calls upon your cash, including out-of-the-blue visits from people who want help, or the need for a temporary home. You could be asked to back a business project or offer a loan or gift.

A home dream could be turned on its head when you are offered a completely different style or location of home to the one you expect. But look again, this could be such good news in disguise. You cannot close your eyes to the negative power at work in a certain family any longer. Are surface appearances worth the hidden heartache?

You need to boost your energy levels, so choose vitamin-rich foods, and eat them raw if possible. Snatched sleep and disturbing dreams leave you exhausted. Try a calming bedtime routine of a warm bath followed by some moments of peaceful thought.

LUCK READING

The colours orange and black are luck-bringers, and this card's number, 16, can make winning wishes come true.

COSMIC COUNSEL

When clouds of change make it hard to see the way ahead, repeat to yourself: "I welcome the unknown, and I will make it work."

the STAR

The shining star offers a symbol of constant confidence and inspiration in the sky, while below a young woman pours water from two vessels, signifying rebirth, renewal and refreshment. This is the card of daring ideas, trust in your own talent and a bright new destiny. And its zodiac links with unorthodox Aquarius underline the theme of remaking life, in a way that can be so good and so healing.

LOVE READING

This card's love-gift is renewed pleasure and sensual passion, even in a relationship that seems to be beyond saving. It can often indicate a return of love after separation or divorce. And its underlying message of second chances and eternal hope also allows partners to let go of damaging memories that keep their romance stuck in stalemate.

Confidence in your power both to attract and to keep the kind of love you need is also indicated. And this translates into a new physical and emotional openness that old – or new – partners will find quite irresistible. Music has special power to inspire and heal within your love-life – play it as loud as you like.

If you are still in search of lasting love, then someone who has experienced similar problems or disappointments in the past can help to heal your heart. And a bond that builds first as friendship may transform itself into really satisfying passion. Look out, too, for a very peaceful face and a quiet, but so sexy, voice. The signs are that someone who is a star in their own world will soon have a place in yours. And together you will achieve wonderful love.

48

LIFE READING

Energy has ebbed away as ideas have come to nothing. But now the Star encourages you to think along new, even outrageous, lines and really get yourself noticed. Right now you have the ability to showcase your true talents in a way that will impress the most demanding of people and pass the most difficult of tests. And yes, this can lead your face, or your voice, to a worldwide audience, however unlikely this seems.

Think positive, this card urges you, because a goal is at last within reach. This may be a job, a home or a family hope. And though one route may be blocked, it is only so that a better and faster one can open up for you. New babies in your life are also strongly indicated.

Protection is a powerful theme within a family – you may be offering it, or receiving it yourself. Either way, it releases an unexpected bond of love that will last a lifetime.

Writing down your dreams will remove their power to frighten you, as you realize which area of your life, or health, they link with. This card is a healing one, and may point to an improvement in a long-term problem or a new approach to helping your own health, through either adding the right things or cutting down on the wrong ones.

LUCK READING

Find fortune in a place where glasses or cameras are sold, and look for number 17, especially against a sky-blue background. Silver and pearl colours are luck-linked, too, plus a place where water flows over pale steps. Note a name you see when you come out of a tunnel – it holds work luck.

COSMIC COUNSEL

When you first wake up, even before you open your eyes, say: "The energy I pour into today will fuel my whole future."

the MOON

The card of hidden emotions. The image of two dogs baying at the Moon represents frustrated and seemingly impossible desire. But the Moon's light can also reveal a great deal. Its link with the star sign of Cancer shows that a tough shell can conceal tender love, and it suggests that illusions need to end. But the liquid dropping from the Moon is also life-nourishing, so all can now begin to go well.

LOVE READING

Your relationships are not yet reaching their potential because your real self is very different from what you, and others, currently believe it to be. You are keeping a safety blanket of ice over your emotions. This may protect you from disappointment, but it blocks out the deeper pleasures of love. Instead of behaving like the dogs howling at the Moon, but from a safe distance, instead of thinking or talking about love, you should let the ice melt and open your heart to real feelings. You do have creative love skills, and a rich and sensual imagination. Now is the time to put them into action.

If you are in a relationship, it is time to talk about what you want. Let your heart reveal the real you and your real desires. And encourage your partner to do the same. There are signs that both you and your partner are hiding what you really feel and that you need to strengthen the love-match by communicating. If a relationship has been troubled by a third person, then this situation is over. But it is important not to dwell on old hurts. If you are looking for love, this card identifies a partner with a strong imagination, whose hobby or career involves writing fiction or designing or selling jewellery. You could meet in a place connected with the word "silver". The twin towers on this card promise that the moonlit night of emotions is preparation for the brightness of the day, and this person will help this happen for you in a fascinating way.

LIFE READING

Ask yourself if you are being honest, with yourself and others, about your working life. You may have smilingly accepted much less than you deserve. You do have special creative talents and are ready to accept responsibility.

Do avoid too many new cash commitments, especially when someone tries to put the squeeze on your emotions. Although you may worry about a member of the family, the past will not repeat itself – unless you let it. You can build the home-life you want, though there are signs that your home lacks the serene colours you need. Try adding some cool blues.

Calm your inner confusion and listen to your body – it is telling you that you need to schedule more time to relax. And remember to eat foods that protect your nerves.

LUCK READING

A contest that is connected to photography could be yours to win. And a surprising invitation to an event such as a film première may be the start of a starry friendship. This card is linked to the number 18, and this could bring you competition luck. It is certainly a good sign when you see it on a blue door or business address linked to a high building.

COSMIC COUNSEL

Every night, just before you go to sleep, repeat this phrase: "I have the special power within me to create a good and loving life."

the SUN

A huge, brilliant sun hangs over the Earth, dropping beads of sparkling dew and brightening and ripening everything – and everyone – beneath it. This is the card of success, clear skies and the promise of a sun-kissed future – your future. Double warmth comes from its astrological link with the Sun, focusing on personal potential and the dazzling light of total self-knowledge – magic luck.

LOVE READING

This card unravels a complicated romance plot and transports you back to a simpler, warmer way of loving. It spells an end to pretence, love-schemes and the kind of heart-deals that bargain with your happiness. Now you find rich romance by being your real self.

Two people who have been separated can soon be reunited again. And this time, work or other practical problems will not come between them. If you are in a relationship, then the signs are that your emotions have matured, and experience has changed your view of love. You appreciate a partner more and understand why certain things had to happen. As a result, deeper commitment looks likely and you are ready to make a set of joint plans – perhaps about children.

If you are seeking love at the moment, drawing the sun card introduces you to someone who is or has been a prize-winner, with strong links to the artistic world and a light, golden touch to their looks. You could meet in a place that starts with "S". The slight down side of this card is an increased appetite both for sensual pleasure and passion intrigue. You may feel that one lover is not enough – but beware. Double-dealing is not for you.

LIFE READING

Drawing this card points you towards fortune, and even fame, in all areas of your life. But you have your part to play – by seizing chances as they come up instead of sitting safe and waiting for something even better. This applies particularly to your working life. You will see one problem in black and white for the first time, as well as the negative influence of one person who is driven by jealousy. But you do have the option of breaking free – careers linked to stage, screen or working with younger people would all work well.

This is an excellent time for trying out daring ideas – perhaps a home decor scheme of pure bright colours, or a brightening up of your own, recently neglected, personal image. Your social life will be extra warm and enjoyable, and place you at the centre of at least one surprise celebration.

If a family has doubted your motives before, this time you will be taken on trust, ending a time of deep suspicion. And a garden or some other piece of shared land can bring a family much closer.

Your body will benefit from warmth and light, so get out and about as much as you can in the open air. And follow up that suggestion of a sunshine break – there is a way to cut the cost.

LUCK READING

Numbers on a screen and questions linked to history can win you cash. And luck will follow when you see number 19 on coloured paper or as a business address. Rooms filled with many mirrors and a man who wears round, gold glasses are lucky.

COSMIC COUNSEL

Imagine the warmth of the sun, first on your face, then seeping through your life, and say: "For every problem, there is a solution."

20 2 △

JUDGEMENT

JUDGEMENT

Decisions may have to be made when you see this card. It is the sign of looking back, perhaps with disappointment, as actions are judged. And then looking forward with new hope. A winged god sounds a trumpet, and earthly beings rise up from their tombs – showing that no situation is final. And links with the generous planet Jupiter underline the themes of judging without blame, changing without fear.

LOVE READING

This is the card of second chances. You may have given up on a relationship, or relationships in general. But drawing this card urges you to think again, to learn from your mistakes rather than letting them defeat you. And you can start by making the first move to clear up misunderstandings – getting back in touch or saying that you are sorry. Or even, if you are free to find love, by approaching that person you sense could be so special and introducing yourself.

If you are already in a relationship, you could be facing several delicate decisions. Believe that you can trust your own judgement – it is wiser and better than any advice from outside. But do be sure you think things through, without letting feelings lead logic astray. Yes, a partner who is not willing, or able, to be fully part of your life may not be the right person for you. And meeting someone with much more warmth and devotion to give could highlight this. You need to make a tough choice, but it will be the right one.

If you are still in search of true love, you will soon receive a phone call or message over the airwaves that takes you to a new place where you meet Mr or Ms Right. This is someone who looks far more serious than they are, and whose work or free time includes some kind of teaching. Take time to let love, and desire, develop slowly, and relish romance that offers mutual support.

LIFE READING

You are entering a time of reckoning, when you must decide who and what you want in your life from now on. Let your mind replay, one last time, the career, cash or home decision you have always regretted. Then release it forever, and replace energy-guzzling regrets with positive ideas and future plans. A time when you have judged yourself and your actions too harshly is over forever. And work paths linked to law and music are opening up.

In your home-life, too, there are changes. These may involve building work or a move to another town, maybe another country. You could also find yourself splitting time between two very different kinds of home.

You will find a special way of helping a family member whose normal routine has been disrupted by ill-health. And look much closer at the needs of children. They do not want your cash, just your time and your attention.

To clear your mind of tiredness, breathe steadily, try gentle, yoga-based exercises and wear shades of blue.

LUCK READING

A place where goods are weighed and prices spoken out loud will set the scene for a rich cash reward. And you will draw success from the number 20 and the colours red and blue. A warm friendship starts from an initial quarrel.

COSMIC COUNSEL

Take time to clear your mind of old doubts and debts, and repeat this: "I will face my past and let it go, ready to seize my future."

the WORLD

A beautiful woman walks free as the air, ringed by a protective laurel wreath of success and guarded by four creatures from different species. This reward card predicts that a whole new world is waiting to open up for you, taking you travelling on both inner and outer journeys. Linked to self-control planet Saturn, the World gives a more grounded, grown-up approach and widens all horizons in your life.

LOVE READING

A very personal cycle of change is coming to its end now. This could be the final phase of an engagement, a pregnancy or even a long legal struggle to start or finish a relationship properly. You will soon be free to move on to the next phase, and put all kinds of plans into action.

If you are in a relationship, then new beginnings is your theme. You may be about to marry, have a child, travel together or start to live a very different kind of shared life. And this will reveal a secret side to both your own love-style and that of a partner. There is so much more there for you to explore, together.

If you are seeking a new partner right now, then someone who has travelled the world, and perhaps speaks with a foreign accent, can be the one. Especially if you meet first through a mix-up with tickets or invitations. This person will help you map out your own love future, and taste the pleasures of a passion that is always changing, always exciting. You may be asked to step into another very different world in order to stay together, and yes, it takes courage. But finding the right love is worth the effort.

LIFE READING

In simple terms, this card may indicate a prolonged spell of worldwide travel, or a new job that involves moving about or following a new route. It is also a strong sign that you do, indeed, have those very talents that you most envy in other people, and must stop thinking of yourself in such a stereotyped, stale way. The time is ideal for you to begin a business, start a course or simply broaden your horizons.

Long-term cash plans pay up very soon, and money may need to be shared in a different, fairer, way. If you have been saving towards a special purchase, you will be ready to spend now.

On the home front, this is a great time for harmony among friends and for sealing rifts that have shattered family links. Someone you really care about shows that your recent efforts to change have been noticed, and it's a good feeling. And some amazing changes, which may include living abroad for part of the year, are in store.

There is a danger of weight gain at the moment – beat this by halving your portions and doubling your intake of fruit and vegetables. A therapy or health book linked to a foreign language can hold the secret of better health for you or someone very close. Do a few minutes gentle stretching every morning.

LUCK READING

Blue and violet, merged in a swirling pattern, signal good luck vibes for you, as does the number 21, especially when it is associated with travel. A contest linked to famous sporting figures, a name spelt out in leaves and artificial grass are further luck links.

COSMIC COUNSEL

At the end of each day, think of everything you would have liked to do differently, and say: "I welcome every chance to grow and learn."

ace of FIRE

ACE of FIRE

This card promises fast-forward action, overnight success, sudden meetings and fire-hot energy.

LOVE READING

If you have an established love-life that lacks the excitement you need, this card shows that it's time to mend it, or bring it to a close. Taking some special time together, even just relaxing at home, can reawaken physical pleasure that's faded. Be open to new ideas.

New love strikes like lightning, in a location linked to the colour red and the letter "A". Light brown hair and a love of daring sports are further pointers. You could be talking marriage – within days!

LIFE READING

Drawing this ace card provides inspiration and originality, but the impetus must come from you. An unusual decorating or design-linked idea can work well, and so can business plans linked to toys or games. There are strong signs of children entering your life in some way. Learn to value relaxation in order to deal with stress.

LUCK READING

Any contest linked to the number 1, or where you are the first contestant, will bring luck your way. Look also for triangle shapes and a well-known food in an orange wrapper.

COSMIC COUNSEL

Say inwardly, "Even mistakes are moving me closer to success."

two of FIRE

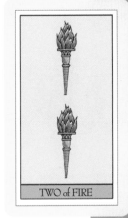

TWO of FIRE

Two brings you partnerships, both love and work ones, shared success and family reunions.

LOVE READING

This is the card of couples, and someone who looks rather like you, or shares your background, could be your perfect pairing. The two is the strongest Tarot signal that love is close, and it will be the kind of deep, doubt-free love you have always dreamed of but never truly dared to try. In a current relationship, this can lead to wild passion that rewrites a shared future. And if you are looking for love, be ready to meet your match playing sport or competing for the same job.

LIFE READING

Someone you see as a rival in fact shares many talents and plans with you. Taking the first step to talk about them may lead you towards a brilliant new work team, especially if there are links to music or medicine. A new practical skill is worth making sacrifices for.

Ice that has frozen up a family link finally starts to thaw, but make absolutely clear what changes you expect, from the start. Spend time each day simply breathing fresh air.

LUCK READING

Sharing an address, even for just a short while, second thoughts about a written answer and a prize trail that links red and blue will all release cash for you. A child's gift enriches a whole family.

COSMIC COUNSEL

Remember these key words: "I must be true to my own ideas."

THREE of FIRE

three of FIRE

Three leads to new love and shared laughter, as drifting ideas develop into an exciting reality.

LOVE READING

You are ready to put past love lessons into practice now. This could mean adding new physical pleasure, or deeper commitment, to a relationship that's been running in neutral lately. Or try talking about the kind of partnership you truly want. Even if a split seems so close, it's not too late to stop it, using this card's powers. Add an element of humour to all you do, and a partner is bound to respond well.

If you are looking for new love, then a voice that draws your attention, in a place where three musicians play, is a strong clue.

LIFE READING

Working in groups of three, perhaps on a stage, could be just the thing for you. But you will need to guard against personal arrogance, or neglecting your family when success arrives. Remember that wealth and fame can never replace the warmth of sincere love.

Don't let pride prevent you from accepting some cash help; this is a time when a deal will go your way. This is also a time for personal growth, including an interesting change of address.

LUCK READING

Arrow shapes, or pointers of some kind, can win prizes for you. Fortune travels towards pyramids in Egypt or South America.

COSMIC COUNSEL

Say: "I will give love without expecting anything back."

four of FIRE

Four is a signal of home and work harmony, new roots and something special to celebrate...

LOVE READING

You are able to heal rifts and end love quarrels, but it may involve a couple moving away from family or work pressures. It will take extra effort on both sides to make love a central theme in your life, instead of letting it fall to the bottom of the list.

If, however, you are giving all your loving to someone who likes to make you feel insecure, then it's time to move on, and access this card's positive love energy. Your dream lover is someone with grey-blue eyes and a talent for drawing portraits.

LIFE READING

New roots at a new address, a boost to earning potential linked to travel, and a new determination to stand firm and face problems instead of fleeing from them – this card shows so much to celebrate! And the key is a more patient, tactful approach to life.

Creative work linked to your own home, or other people's, can push you into the success zone. You could even live abroad for a while. Choose exercise you enjoy to reap the best benefits.

LUCK READING

Returning a set of keys, or something linked to animals, starts money flowing your way. Luck links you to someone who wears a family heirloom ring. Pressing buttons helps you to win prizes.

COSMIC COUNSEL

Before sleeping, say: "I am ready to take control of my own life."

FIVE of FIRE

five of FIRE

Five spells challenges and prizes that are well worth striving for. This is the card of competition.

LOVE READING

Love tensions can disappear – once you decide to put up a fight. And this can be for your own needs, your own rights, or against a rival who at first seems like a special friend. Remember, this person's only weapons are words, and refuse to let yourself be wounded or manipulated.

This card is telling you that love can overcome any barriers it faces – provided that the love is real. If you are still a love-seeker, a role in a sports team, or the fitness world, is your way in. Look past a seemingly loud personality to quiet tenderness.

LIFE READING

This card's challenge is to fight for changes that you want. At home and at work it's important to turn anger into good energy. But do resist being rushed to new places that don't feel right.

Finances are rocked, but not capsized, by the pleasure plans of someone close. Five people who dress alike are a key to new cash. Calm your mind with time out for steady breathing.

LUCK READING

Contests that pitch your physical skills against someone else, or test your knowledge of television, bring prizes of cash or travel. When a family debt is repaid in an intriguing way, it leads to luck.

COSMIC COUNSEL

Tell yourself: "I focus on my good future by letting the past go."

six of FIRE

Six shows how flexibility leads to fortune, hard work is repaid and good news is on the way.

SIX of FIRE

LOVE READING

This card of reversal often predicts a marriage or reunion at a time when all hope was fading. If you've put hard work into a difficult relationship, you'll be repaid by some breakthrough news and will see that your trust was not misplaced.

The sudden wedding of someone close could be a turning point for you. New love speaks with a strong accent and number 6 features in his or her age. Be flexible and understanding.

LIFE READING

Ambition burns far brighter than you admit – now your true aims can find expression, with faraway travel as part of the deal.

Foreign food, a lawyer with a most unusual name, and photographs of your home, or something in it, combine to turn old doubts into new security. And it will access all areas of your life. A family's future is decided at last – in your favour. But even good times can be stressful, so eat when you're calm, to avoid digestive problems.

LUCK READING

Number 6 linked to a car could lead to an exotic, last-minute trip, and big prizes are possible in contests that involve making yourself look, or dress, in a different way, or rearranging letters or pictures. Someone close gives up a plan for you, and gains a great deal.

COSMIC COUNSEL

Tell yourself: "I must trust myself so that I can trust others."

seven of FIRE

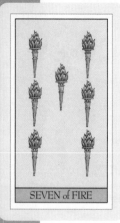

SEVEN of FIRE

Seven signals a mix of daring and caring, dealing with problems, and refreshing life change.

LOVE READING

Smooth success is not for you in love – you need challenges to secure the strong, passionate partnership you deserve. A new potential partner is someone who works, or spends a lot of time, outdoors, and who will test your love in tantalizing ways. You could meet at a local quiz, or when you share the same puzzle on a journey or in a waiting room. An established love benefits when you break free of routine roles and add daring to your caring. Your best hope of happiness is honesty.

LIFE READING

Facing up to a secret fear will transform your life and your working world. An extra dose of determination helps you to crush competition and win a job with extra cash and better conditions. Success is linked to sharing knowledge, skills or experience.

A new slant on an old game, and a hobby linked to hills or mountains, can make money. When a visitor stays longer than expected, home changes may start. Avoid too much caffeine.

LUCK READING

Travel is your luck-ticket, but personal happiness centres on your home, and following your own ideas. Animals, answering radio questions, and a one-off work offer are also lucky for you.

COSMIC COUNSEL

Say: "I do deserve the good things in my life."

eight of FIRE

Eight outlines a life that speeds up and whisks you far away, reaching out to hope and happiness.

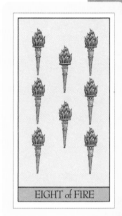

LOVE READING

New love will rush into your life with the heat of a volcano – either with a current partner or with someone totally new and different, whose eyes suddenly lock on yours as you travel towards a work or home change. There are signs of a double life – a serious job by day, chasing fame as an entertainer by night. And shared laughter will be a big part of your relationship, and help to lighten those moods.

If you are already in a relationship, stop hiding your warmth and physical passion. Showing need will help love to grow strong.

LIFE READING

This is the card that shows delays coming to an end, and money matters swinging your way. And a trip back in time to an old school or home brings a rich bonus. Your special way of looking at the world in both words and pictures could result in a job.

Just because a family expects you to react in one way doesn't mean you can't choose another path. Your wheel of health currently needs a good push – walking every day will certainly help.

LUCK READING

Boats, and contests on or near water, are luck-bringers. So is meeting at a table set for eight and a gold-edged card.

COSMIC COUNSEL

Make this your secret slogan: "I can create my own success."

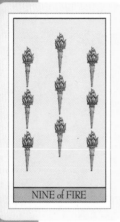

NINE of FIRE

nine of FIRE

Nine helps you to look deeper into your hopes, and your heart, and find healing inner strengths.

LOVE READING

Silence makes love differences grow greater. Over the next nine weeks, please take time to work through these differences together, and break the shadowy spell of past problems and disappointments. Established love can be so strong and exciting again.

New love could start now with someone who uses special insight in his or her job, perhaps as a detective or a counsellor.

LIFE READING

It's time to discover your talents for writing and designing – the greetings card business would be an excellent path to try. And someone who sells paintings, or teaches painting, can be a lifelong luck link, starting now.

Cash matters can be complex – you are asked to finish someone else's project, and given very little time. But the results will be worthwhile. Do guard against greediness in a family share-out, perhaps linked to insurance, and give help without ever judging. Alternative medicine could make a minor problem disappear.

LUCK READING

A child's words or picture pushes you towards prizes, and your instinct about an object's worth is correct – let experts confirm it.

COSMIC COUNSEL

Say to yourself: "I am moving forward with much confidence."

ten of FIRE

Ten tells you to expect success, but with responsibility and power that must be controlled.

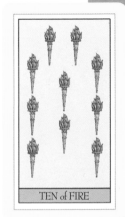

TEN of FIRE

LOVE READING

One side of a couple is about to enjoy tremendous success, and become richer in so many ways. But this may cause problems for the other partner — something both sides should be aware of. Love responsibility means refusing to use physical or emotional power to push a partnership in the wrong direction, and sometimes accepting restrictions on freedom. Then all will go well.

If you are searching for love, focus on someone with close-cut hair, who works at night and speaks in a very frank way.

LIFE READING

A difficult or dark time is drawing to a close. You can speed this up by taking firm action, which may mean dropping a secret scheme — forever. If your wish for a family or work team to be reunited can't come true, then please say yes to a new group.

Don't spend so much energy and cash fighting against a change that is already happening. Focus instead on a business idea, linked to emergency situations, that is about to take off. A health matter will make steady progress from now on.

LUCK READING

Events that feature fireworks or coloured lights mark cash luck.

COSMIC COUNSEL

Repeat to yourself: "Kindness, not force, will take me to the top."

FIRE PRINCESS

fire PRINCESS

The Princess's promise is a new lease of life and love, as well as invigorating, fire-bright energy.

LOVE READING

Get ready to feel the thrills and spills of love's rollercoaster – whatever age you are. However long you've been in a relationship, it's as if you've only just begun. And activities or holidays in the open air are important keys.

The new love-match that this card maps out for you is someone young in mind and brave in spirit, who lives a very physical life, perhaps linked to their work. Your love-life will be a little quirky and rich in physical satisfaction.

LIFE READING

Money, or a skill, will pass from one generation of a family to another, and a secret talent for tracing family trees, or other paths through history, could be the career switch you need. You may need to change plans, or even your address, very quickly.

Better work co-operation, success in a special test or interview and an exciting message linked to a young, pushy woman with red hair, all chase away past work doubts. Plan your days better to allow enough time for rest, relaxation and gentle exercise.

LUCK READING

A team of people, all under 21, plus a visitor from abroad, help you towards a money prize. So does a list of exotic place-names.

COSMIC COUNSEL

Repeat: "My future looks good, I refuse to waste time on regrets."

fire PRINCE

The Prince brings startling, satisfying events, like a torch of fire leading to brighter times.

FIRE PRINCE

LOVE READING

A person who makes you smile, then reaches your heart so tenderly, could be your perfect partner. This could also be someone whose job involves speaking, or writing, funny lines. You will step into a new, exciting life together, after meeting in a place linked with travel. This card also promises new thrills and adventures in an existing love. The key is acting out new love roles that allow your many passion personalities to show.

LIFE READING

Put a joint money plan on hold for now – you still have so much excitement to get out of your system. This is a lively, restless period, when ideas and offers are all around you. Do take up some of these when you reach a work crossroads – an instinct that is pushing you towards the world of advertising is just the thing for you.

Get a journey, either emotional or physical, over with soon – a home goal that is within your grasp needs you to feel more settled. Boost health with dried fruit.

LUCK READING

A young man who talks a lot, and likes very unusual music, is one cash key, plus a local theatre group and a meeting at a barbecue.

COSMIC COUNSEL

Say it, and believe it: "I have confidence in my own instincts."

FIRE QUEEN

fire QUEEN

The Queen represents kindness, sympathy, open emotion and a rich flame of natural growth.

LOVE READING

A warm, wise woman with many different links to children could act as a matchmaker in your love-life – and the partner she chooses may start off as a work colleague. You will recognize your match by brightly coloured clothes and a name of foreign origin, as well as a sharp brain.

A relationship that has become unbalanced, with one partner doing too much of the love-work, can be corrected. But this can only be done by having a rethink of your responsibilities and your approach to romance that will help you to turn fantasy into reality.

LIFE READING

Someone really close to you is facing a difficult choice, with echoes of your own past. If you know the answer, please reveal it gently, but firmly. Stop false hope now, before it goes too far.

A time when you have felt unsettled right across your life is ending, and a woman who hides a tender heart under a mask of sarcasm could be the key to new work power. Dancing and selling clothes are both rich in opportunity for you. Exercising in a group setting brings social and physical benefits.

LUCK READING

A journey south, and blue and yellow on china, lead to luck.

COSMIC COUNSEL

Repeat three times a day: "The love I give will be rewarded."

fire KING

The King shows that the loyalty and generosity you give, and receive, light your way to success.

LOVE READING

Someone older, and in a position of power, will break through your fear that you will never be loved as you truly want to be. Your heart will now be brave and you will feel so much more attractive. In a relationship, this leads to letting a bad memory go – this time for good – and unlocks exotic, uninhibited passion skills that leave a partner reeling.

Someone with dark hair, deep-set eyes and a famous surname can bring bright-burning new love to you. You'll meet in a room decorated in Eastern style, at an event linked to local business.

LIFE READING

Managing a sports team, or a singing group, could be on your work agenda when someone with great influence spots special potential in you. Creative ideas are really strong, and so is your need, and ability, to make a home the happy, co-operative place you dream of.

Cash chances depend on your own attitude – act optimistic, even if you feel the opposite, and a situation will start to move in the right direction. Work that gives more contact with the public could go especially well. Beware of setting exercise standards too high.

LUCK READING

Trips to famous houses or gardens put you in line for prizes.

COSMIC COUNSEL

Your personal watchword is: "Every challenge leaves me stronger."

71

ace of EARTH

ACE of EARTH

The capable and practical ace of earth promises progress, profit, safety and unity across your life.

LOVE READING

Drawing the ace card flicks a switch on a new way of looking at love – are you putting financial security before the happiness of your heart? Too much work, and too much worry, eat away at passion, so do try to make more time for a partner. There are many dreams that are within reach, and many decisions that should not be put off for some richer future. If you are looking for love, someone who wears a single piece of gold can offer passion and stability.

LIFE READING

This is a card of renewal, and it can signify a family drawing close again, perhaps through a birth or a remarriage. Business projects thrive. And you will be helped by a cash gift that links to a period in your life that you would rather forget. Boost your health by increasing air circulation in your home.

LUCK READING

Spring-cleaning your life, both emotionally and practically, brings luck back. So do contests connected to cleaning materials, a sudden switch of travel plans, and the number 37.

COSMIC COUNSEL

Tell yourself: "I welcome change and I know all will go well."

two of EARTH

Two copes with challenges and problems, achieving balance through a flexible approach.

TWO of EARTH

LOVE READING

Organization is the key to deeper, stronger loving. If you are a love-seeker, then someone with a very solid, practical approach to life deserves a special place in your heart. By taking over routine problems that sap your energy, this person leaves much more room for romance. And a time when your heart has been scared to make that big step ends.

If you are already in a relationship, then you are the one who must reorganize your love-life. Passion is not being shared equally.

LIFE READING

If you have been either over-stretching yourself or setting too-strict work limits, now's the time to stop. This may mean dropping one cash plan or partnership that weighs heavily on your heart. But it also opens the door to a new team linked with travel.

Remember that it is richness of feelings, not furnishings, that makes a home happy – family needs are changing so much at the moment. Gentle stretching exercises, letting yourself laugh, and limiting tea and coffee will soothe stress.

LUCK READING

Family house names or numbers are circled with gold, and you make a lucky move by welcoming an extra person into your home.

COSMIC COUNSEL

Make your motto: "Sometimes I must let my heart rule my head."

three of EARTH

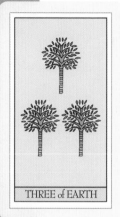

THREE of EARTH

Three of earth signals that hard work is rewarded, and a more practical approach clinches a property deal.

LOVE READING

Too much thought and too little action is dulling your love instincts. Passion alone is not enough – you must add a helping of simple friendship and shared planning to move a relationship on. Don't be afraid to speak out first, your ideas will be very well received. Surround yourself with sensual fabrics and soft lighting to create an irresistible love mood.

If you are looking for love, then someone who is very fair, and has links to children's health, is the right one. You could meet a destiny partner in a place where healthy eating advice is given.

LIFE READING

You could reap rich rewards from the beauty or photographic business. It may be hard to accept new restrictions on your life, or your imagination, but it will be worth it in the long term.

A third meeting, or a meeting where three people are present, will seal a property deal. Do not close your mind to outside help with a family problem – it could be the deciding factor. Food or drink may offer comfort, but it's better to face up to the problem.

LUCK READING

A coupon or entry form in three parts is a key to new luck.

COSMIC COUNSEL

Repeat to yourself daily: "I am ready now to let love fill my life."

four of EARTH

Four says too much security can be as dangerous as too little – let more spontaneity into your life!

FOUR of EARTH

LOVE READING

This card shows a strong and steady love, either in a current relationship or in one about to begin or begin again. But there is a danger that the edge of attraction between two people will be blunted by one partner, or both, being too obsessed with cash. Take time to make exciting plans for both partners' physical pleasure and fantasies, as well as bank accounts, in order to keep passion fresh.

If you seek love, you could face a choice between someone who offers wealth, but could starve your heart, and another person who loves generously and has a job or hobby linked to gardens.

LIFE READING

Instant results are not likely on the home front, but long-term goals are well within your reach. So it's time to put over-ambitious property plans on hold. Ask yourself why a house does not feel like a home. Do you see it only as a prize, or a means to profit?

Letting your feelings out – yes, even the negative ones – will benefit both your family relationships and your health. And it will also free lots of energy. Use this to tackle new cash challenges.

LUCK READING

Contests that involve moving or examining coins are winners.

COSMIC COUNSEL

Repeat to yourself: "I respect my own needs and reach out to life."

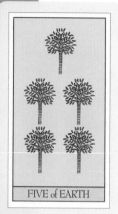

FIVE of EARTH

five of EARTH

Five is not easy, but it is rewarding. It shows a gap in your life – and a choice of how to fill it.

LOVE READING

Anxiety over love can keep emotions frozen – worry over what might go wrong combines with regrets over past mistakes to paralyze even the most open hearts and minds. And this can lead to deeply unsatisfying relationships. Please focus on what is good in your present love-life and how you can make it even better. And, if instincts tell you that the only answer is to take time apart, don't be afraid to follow them.

If you are looking for love, destiny sends you someone with close connections to a cold country and the initial "N" or "W".

LIFE READING

There can be a cash loss or delay indicated by this card – but it is one that will leave you richer personally. Someone whose support you seek could be a loyal friend for life and teach you the kind of calm organization that brings back security.

Work that has never really felt right can be changed for a new career path – a building with round windows is a strong clue. Don't give up on a health plan, success will come some time in the next few weeks.

LUCK READING

The return of a lost item is ringed with special luck for you.

COSMIC COUNSEL

Remember this: "I meet every challenge with a welcoming smile."

six of EARTH

Six says that the more you give, the more you get – problems are solved and joy is shared.

LOVE READING

If you think that love has been going well, it's about to get even better! However long a relationship has survived, it is poised to enter its most thrilling, sensual phase ever. And you are at the centre of the action, finding exciting ways to make love feel new and special. Sharing your deepest doubts, perhaps linked to a shadow from the past, leaves both sides lighter. And a partner is happy for you to set the passion pace, with interesting results.

If you are still seeking lasting love, then someone you work or study with, as well as writing with unusual loops, are hot clues.

LIFE READING

A sum of cash is coming soon. However tempting it is to keep it all, it must be shared out fairly. Your key to lasting luck is opening up communication channels again, especially with children.

Look closer at a kind of work that involves speaking up for others' talents or rights. A lighter, brighter atmosphere rules at home, and postponed projects or moving plans get going again. Tackling life one day at a time soothes anxiety.

LUCK READING

Gifts wrapped in shiny paper and June birthdays are your luck signs.

COSMIC COUNSEL

Repeat: "My life is filled up with joy, as I release worry."

SEVEN of EARTH

seven of EARTH

Seven sees good results. Losses turn into gains, friendship into passion. Perseverance pays off.

LOVE READING

If you think romance has left your life, think again – for however rocky a relationship has been, it is about to get a real boost, both physically and emotionally. What you must do is change your attitude. Stop seeing disappointment as defeat, and show confidence in yourself and in love.

A friend, or a lover who has come to feel like a friend, can develop into your true passion destiny. If you are single, other clues are a job or hobby filled with daily danger and a special courage that has helped overcome a physical challenge.

LIFE READING

A job that links you to helping others, either by sharing knowledge or supplying skills, would be perfect for you. And this step can happen, once you decide to stop letting doubts from the past drag you down. This may mean a trip back towards a person or a place that holds bad memories, but the outcome will be positive.

One person's needs are stifling a family – it's time to speak out. Physical symptoms are linked to over-stretching your mind.

LUCK READING

Tests of knowledge and strength are your fortune-finders.

COSMIC COUNSEL

Say: "When I show that I value myself, others value me, too."

eight of EARTH

EIGHT of EARTH

Eight is a strong symbol of both financial and emotional support, promotion and practical ideas.

LOVE READING

Love-seekers, look no further! This card shows that the perfect partner for you is someone who has won, or been given, a brilliant cash chance, and chooses to spend some of it helping others on a local level. This will be a love-match that mixes down-to-earth physical expression with a spiritual element where two hearts and two minds recognize each other instantly.

If you are already matched, then this card indicates that one partner is changing, and both need to modify their love.

LIFE READING

This is the talent card, and shows that you will soon recognize, and use, hidden or forgotten skills. And there are strong signs that this could lead to your own business, or a big promotion.

Stubborn opinions could divide a family – forcing the issue is not the answer; pursuing your own personal ideas is. Home luck is linked to someone with lots of books, and letting go of sentimental objects. Accepting natural changes helps health.

LUCK READING

Changing a room around, a film star's face, and making a journey you've always dreaded bring luck, along with the power of 44.

COSMIC COUNSEL

Breathe deeply and repeat: "I can create the life I want."

NINE of EARTH

nine of EARTH

Nine promises a home enriched by wealth and wisdom, problems solved and queries answered.

LOVE READING

Dark hair and darker eyes introduce new love. The ninth time you meet will change your life. If you are in a relationship, a time of false love, when neither side has dared to show real feelings or real doubts, is ending. And your mutual passion will be richer for this helping of reality. Let out some of your hidden love fantasies... a partner will be fascinated.

LIFE READING

Home and work do not mix right now – keep them separate. But property is poised to play a vital part in your destiny. First, through the legacy of a house, or a share of a house, that has special value to industry. And second, through a project that's been on hold for a long time – a project that will build the kind of home you deserve.

When family members join together to raise cash for a good cause, it heals the hurt of resentment that has created such chills lately. Better-spaced and planned meals, especially breakfast, could boost energy levels back to normal. Try to avoid smoky areas.

LUCK READING

Identifying famous buildings or landmarks is your main prize-finder, plus invitations edged with gold, and the initial "R".

COSMIC COUNSEL

Remember: "Wishes coming from the heart can come true."

ten of EARTH

TEN of EARTH

Solid foundations underline ten's theme – of marriage, family life, friendship and future career.

LOVE READING

Passion that has been so near, yet separated from you by a series of upsets and worries, could be ready to come into your life. If you are in a relationship, then this powerful sign of weddings, christenings and other family celebrations promises new stability and shared plans for a rock-solid future.

Even the most difficult of cash problems can now be solved, but you must play your part. Reject resentment and bitter blame and believe in a partner's new self. If you are looking for love, a name starting with "A" is a strong clue, along with looks that match yours.

LIFE READING

You can be a player in the fame game, through a talent for advising others. And any work idea that links to a member of your family, or to someone who shares the same name, signs you up for success. But beware of showing your feelings on your face. Let a calm smile cover all strong emotions, good and bad.

This is the family focus card and it promises a special bond with a recent family arrival. Steer clear of very strong tastes in food.

LUCK READING

Identifying fragments of music or of a picture brings prizes.

COSMIC COUNSEL

Hold in your heart: "I expect love, and this attracts love to me."

EARTH PRINCESS

earth PRINCESS

Steady progress at work and in love, sensual discovery and a chance to travel are close at hand.

LOVE READING

Someone you meet seems so quiet at first, yet under that conventional surface is a romantic and responsive lover, with just the loyalty that has been lacking in your life. If you are looking for a new relationship, this could happen with someone you see daily, perhaps on a journey. And a link to some kind of keyboard is likely.

If you are already in an established partnership, then getting back to basics and rediscovering each other is the key to happiness. Take nothing for granted and rebuild trust from the beginning.

LIFE READING

It's not changing your skills that brings a new work start, but applying them in a different way, or in a different setting. And this could mean regular foreign travel or communicating in another language. Travel also helps to sharpen your personal insight.

Accept that this is the time for big changes to happen to someone close, and your chance will come too, when you are ready. Guard against over-stretching your physical ability and look out for a new address with links to a royal family.

LUCK READING

Choose contests that run over several weeks and are linked to shops.

COSMIC COUNSEL

Repeat often to yourself: "I do not need to settle for second best."

earth PRINCE

EARTH PRINCE

As well as showing respect, achievement and energy, this card creates positive personal change.

LOVE READING

As a symbol of high energy, this card suggests that one side of a relationship may be investing too much energy in entertainment, leaving love to wither away. But ignoring this won't help. If you express your feelings fully and honestly, then any barrier to love will lift and new trust and passion will develop. Sharing an activity like exercise, or something artistic, is a good start.

If you are looking for love, someone who has dedicated their life to a career or a cause could be the one. But you need to get past a tough outer shell that scares most people away. Dark hair and a lot of friends in the sporting world are further specific clues.

LIFE READING

The person who will figure strongly in your finances should be someone younger, who uses a lot of jargon or technical terms, and who will work hard to improve your cash prospects. Big family changes are indicated, but don't be lured into over-commitment by tempting printed words. See a health plan through properly.

LUCK READING

Bright waistcoats, cities starting with the letter "S", the number 48, and contests linked to physical strength form your luck list.

COSMIC COUNSEL

This must be your motto: "I am not afraid to try new things."

83

EARTH QUEEN

earth QUEEN

The Queen signifies home comforts, the beauty of nature, earthy sexuality and fertility.

LOVE READING

Someone whom you first see on television talking about food or the home could turn up in your real life and make special contact that speaks straight to your heart. And so a love starts that is gentle yet strong; stable yet thrillingly sexy.

If you are in a relationship, then a period of loneliness or disappointment is about to disappear. It will be replaced by a warmer, more home-based love that makes the same demands of both sides. A baby plan could move from dream to reality.

LIFE READING

Writing about food, or making it in a special setting, might be the key to work success – this card also signals a connection with a hot climate. But you do need to approach work with a lighter touch, then you'll find that truly creative talents can shine through.

At home, someone having a tough time linked to children needs to talk, but do take it slowly. This is the card of home and hearth happiness and does promise a calm time – linked to people, not possessions. But be wary of boredom bringing bad eating habits.

LUCK READING

Jewellery, and contests linked to menus, are luck-linked.

COSMIC COUNSEL

Repeat it, and really believe it: "Love grows when it is shared."

earth KING

The King sees life's unsung luxuries – good, lasting love, useful skills, comfort and patience.

LOVE READING

You see someone who looks so much like your dream lover that it's a shock. However shy you feel, you must approach this person. Words and feelings will flow, and a perfect partnership will begin. Be ready in a place linked with medicine.

If you are in a relationship right now, then there may be a shadow of doubt that one partner treats the other like a possession, or lets work take up too much time. This situation can change when two people really talk and stir up the embers of old emotion.

LIFE READING

A link with an older man, perhaps a relative, is a rich one for you in two ways. First, it matches your practical plans with his imagination. Second, he turns a business idea into action.

Family money comes from a land-linked legacy, and, at home, accepting the relationships you have, rather than fantasizing about the perfect family, brings some good changes. Each day, take 20 minutes alone to count down to complete calm.

LUCK READING

Choose contests with an historical flavour, or linked to the healing world.

COSMIC COUNSEL

Place this idea in your mind: "I release the past and find peace."

85

THE SUIT OF AIR

ACE of AIR

ace of AIR

Love and ideas strike your life like lightning with this major indicator of brilliant mind-power.

LOVE READING

Instant, irresistible attraction is so close now, and the source is someone with a high-speed lifestyle and links to the screen who will ask for promises of passion and snap decisions from you. But this love could mean leaving behind the life you have built up. Thrilling, certainly; secure – never.

In a settled relationship, danger flashes when partners assume that they know everything about each other. Use your mental strength and show your personality more to keep a lover guessing.

LIFE READING

At work, tempers may spark, but you have the ideas needed to reunite a team. The ace shines out as a sign of original thinking, and any venture you start, or object you invent, will make a real impact. Sudden decisions and new directions are indicated here.

You will also take a special supportive role when a child who is extremely close finds fame very young. Check all use-by labels.

LUCK READING

Helping someone to recover, mentally or physically, is linked to luck, along with yellow, the number 10 and contests linked to drinks.

COSMIC COUNSEL

Say quietly each day: "I welcome all opportunities in my life."

two of AIR

Two brings opposite sides and ideas together, and promises to double your share of passion.

TWO of AIR

LOVE READING

Get set to be at the centre of a love battle – and the prize will be your heart. You'll meet one would-be lover in a place where two very different local sides compete. And the other is someone already in your life, who often asks your opinion about music. It may seem impossible to choose, but tune into your mind and you will know the right answer.

If you are in a relationship, make time together a priority and bring two minds and bodies back in step with each other.

LIFE READING

You have such a talent for bringing two sides of a quarrel together that you should seriously think about work as a counsellor, either in a business or personal setting. Cash concerns that have weighed on your mind are not unchangeable. Take the first step today.

Power in a family can be shared, but not in a way that will please everyone, so stop trying. A double home choice throws open an exciting new horizon. Smile more, always eat breakfast, and massage the soles of your feet to release tension.

LUCK READING

Look for number 42 and matching two halves of a face or object.

COSMIC COUNSEL

Say: "I can express my anger, and joy, in good and open ways."

THREE of AIR

three of AIR

Difficult situations are swept away and good feelings rule, as three is a healing, helping card.

LOVE READING

A relationship is ready to move on to a new phase – ask yourself why you are resisting. If love stays static, it will stagnate. Face the doubts in your mind, then let them go. And tap into a partner's secret weakness – love words whispered in a foreign language.

If you are looking for love, ditch sad or angry feelings that stop you trusting in togetherness. Then you will be ready to meet someone with dark hair and a flair for unusual painting.

LIFE READING

Demands are being made on you now, but soon the situation will be reversed, and you will be the winner. Turn jealousy or frustration at work into positive change by tackling a trouble-maker and asking for a solution that will work.

You have great courage and confidence in a crisis and could be offered the kind of career that suits this, perhaps in the emergency services. Cash is tied up in a triangle of three people or places, but you can free it now.

LUCK READING

Aeroplanes, triangles and someone who has just left a business or pleasure partnership are lucky. So is answering against the clock.

COSMIC COUNSEL

Assure yourself: "I give myself permission to be who I really am."

four of AIR

Four is a card of recovery and rebuilding, a symbol of peace, love and positive reactions.

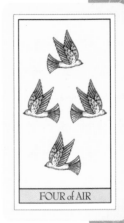

FOUR of AIR

LOVE READING

Someone who looks glamorous, yet works with total dedication in a caring career, could be your destiny lover. And you will meet at an event with links to medicine. Drawing this card shows that recent storms or disappointments in your emotional life have blown over for good, and a gentler, safer period is starting.

If you are settled in a relationship, time apart could be the key to getting troubles in perspective. And words spoken or read by a third person may make a couple rethink a very final decision.

LIFE READING

There is a stream of money ready to flow into your life, and you should use it to fulfil a childhood dream that is still really special. Reopening ties from the past, both business and pleasure, is starred for success, but do work at staying flexible.

Writing and presenting ideas, either your own or other people's, could prove very rewarding. Creating a special space for yourself at home, away from others' problems, is a health plus.

LUCK READING

The fourth time you ask for a decision or a promise will be the one that changes your life. Blue lines are lucky, too.

COSMIC COUNSEL

Say slowly: "I set my mind free to give myself the best choices."

five of AIR

This is the card of strong resolve, will-power and stamina. Five says you're in charge!

LOVE READING

If your heart has been caught in a trap of one-way love, you can break free now, and put mental space between you and a partner. Then, in a cool, calm way, ask for what you want. This card shows that it's never too late to change the rules, or the atmosphere, of a relationship.

Looking for new love? Then someone with a famous name, who has a job that involves addressing an audience, is the right one.

LIFE READING

Don't let last-minute nerves snatch away a home- or job-switch that is just what you need. It's daunting, but you can do it. And if you don't try this time, you may really regret it. Social or family success stirs up old rivalries that need careful handling – remember to share your happiness without showing off. A family's future could involve either a home, or large chunks of time, abroad.

Focus on what you can achieve, not what you can't. A recurring medical problem needs proper information and advice. Sleep for at least seven hours a night and life will look bright again.

LUCK READING

Contests with air tickets as prizes, matching dates to events and joining a sports outing of five are all luck-bringers.

COSMIC COUNSEL

Advise yourself daily: "I let the past go to strengthen the future."

six of AIR

SIX of AIR

Six is the card that shows you taking control. It is the emblem of creating order out of chaos.

LOVE READING

A relationship can be all you hope for – if you add a bit of balance. Until now, you have let someone take too much control, accepted too much and asserted yourself too little. Now you are in charge, and have the extra sharpness and strength needed to turn love around.

If you are still seeking love, choose someone you first meet when he or she is talking about adventures abroad.

LIFE READING

A long-running conflict at work can turn into co-operation instead, and suddenly two enemies find themselves working really closely and well together. This is a card with a strong travel indicator, so any job linked to holidays or transport could suit.

Don't worry about revising a cash agreement several times – it's worth waiting to get it absolutely right. Being invited into a new circle of people, perhaps someone else's family, sparks a fresh outlook on problems, and even solves a few. A family is on the move – not far in terms of distance, but a long way in terms of life-style.

LUCK READING

Winnings centre on mazes, physical tests and sports with high barriers, as well as a new route on a regular journey.

COSMIC COUNSEL

Say this phrase: "I choose the thoughts that make me feel good."

SEVEN of AIR

seven of AIR

This shows unexpected victory, ideas turned into action and holidays turned into honeymoons.

LOVE READING

A situation that has kept two people apart is changing, for the best. Feelings that were unsure are solid now, and you have the ability to talk your way through opposition, either from family or from your own super-cautious side. Add a rare gift for expressing love in warm ways and what starts as a holiday could switch to a first – or second – honeymoon.

However unlikely it seems, if new romance is what you want, it is very close – and it will be with someone who seems to read your thoughts, but does not reveal much about his or her past.

LIFE READING

This is an action card, so choose your projects with care as they could happen very fast. An old work colleague or neighbour can open new work doors for you – within seven weeks you could be your own boss. But choose the straight way forward – no short cuts!

You can also get some cash back, even from high places. A family is strained by one person's unfinished projects and relationships, so speak out. Massage your shoulders to ease tension.

LUCK READING

Fortune flies high where coloured flags are in the air. A bargain bought by someone else and a house reached by seven steps add luck.

COSMIC COUNSEL

Say to yourself: "I know my decisions are the right ones for me."

eight of AIR

False faces and false starts are in the past with the eight of air, which sharpens mind-skills, too.

EIGHT of AIR

LOVE READING

If you feel that love has started so well, so often, but never really reached your goals, then that is about to change. This is a card of making clean breaks with the past – instead of letting venom from bad memories destroy your trust.

A relationship will bloom again when you reach out and show you have put the past behind you, forever. New love is strongly indicated too. All pointers indicate someone with a sharp mind, who may use it in some sort of detective work.

LIFE READING

If your life has been ruled by one relative with strong views, now is the time to say firmly how you feel. Your mind is growing sharper each day, ready for challenges ahead. Don't let routine cash problems pull your attention away from a sudden golden opportunity.

You have a special gift for presenting words or pictures in a way that people really enjoy. Channel it into the publishing world. Home changes can happen with help from someone you have never really liked. Look deeper to realize that you were wrong.

LUCK READING

Games that test mental skill and word-power, plus a news or film quiz, spell luck. Knowledge of a city abroad is a winner.

COSMIC COUNSEL

Repeat: "When truth and love guide my choices, all will go well."

nine of AIR

NINE of AIR

Nine is the card of passing tests, of learning patience, and repairing broken hearts and homes.

LOVE READING

However much you want to seize the love moment, right now you have to sit tight and wait for someone else to make a move. This gives you time to really think about what you want, and need, from a relationship. And you should see finally that any doubts about love come only from your own head. It won't be easy to wait, but it will be worth it.

If you are still seeking your destiny partner, someone who has very strong, but unusual, beliefs could be the right choice.

LIFE READING

Rip off the mask of old malice, and look again at a family situation. It can be improved, even transformed, but you need to make some moves very soon. Your name is high on a secret selection list, and the subject may be home, work, or both. And even if you've rejected a request to travel towards a new, simpler, kind of life before, this time the deal is very different.

Cash comes from two very separate sources – both linked to the letter "I". Don't get caught in the middle of a friend's fight.

LUCK READING

An address where lots of pictures are on show is lucky, along with recipes and musical scores. A cashpoint chat could change your life.

COSMIC COUNSEL

Repeat this: "My dreams hold the truth about who I can be."

ten of AIR

A life heading towards the light, simple pleasures and problems solved are the theme of card ten.

TEN of AIR

LOVE READING

You are about to share in a strong, true love that cancels out even the bitterest of memories. If you are in a relationship, then you can really share love with your partner if you both turn from broken promises and fantasy hopes and focus on what is good between you.

You and your partner may be making a break that takes both of you away from the pressure of family, and personality-changing habits may be in the air. You will find that love shines like new once again. Fate is finding you a mate right now – and it is someone you first see giving something away.

LIFE READING

Two families decide to talk again, and you are in the middle. Cut through cluttered chat to clean, fast action, and put a plan on the table. If work worries have sliced too deeply into your time, or made you postpone a child-linked decision, then this situation is ending now. You are moving towards a simpler, less crowded life.

Cash loss can turn to gain with one clever question – so ask it. Soothe tension with mood-balancing aromatherapy oils.

LUCK READING

Luck comes from garden names, pictures of plants and number 46.

COSMIC COUNSEL

Say quietly: "Not one of my problems is without a solution."

AIR PRINCESS

air PRINCESS

Emotional fire under a calm surface, the Princess promises challenging love and a rebirth of hope.

LOVE READING

If you are looking for new love, then you will respond to someone younger, with elegant cheekbones and a lightning-fast brain. At first you may feel daunted by this intelligence, and by this person's job, which involves teaching adults, but soon you will see the empty space in his or her life – which you alone are needed to fill.

In a current relationship, you are entering a time for fresh love negotiations. Powerful feelings and unstable moods leave love shaky – you can control these, but you do need support.

LIFE READING

Drawing this card often indicates that you have, in the past, missed out on learning. But it's never too late to rethink your working life. You are highly observant and have real skills in arguing for others – abilities that would make you a great researcher, teacher or lawyer, whatever your age.

At home, when opinions differ, the youngest person is right. Two people who look really alike are the key to new cash.

LUCK READING

Contests that pair similar pictures, visiting a twinned town, and mixed-up music bring luck – plus the number 47.

COSMIC COUNSEL

Promise yourself: "I release worry and start my happier life now."

air PRINCE

The Prince pushes fear away and acts fast. This is a card of calm courage and deep creativity.

AIR PRINCE

LOVE READING

Yes, you can ask that love question now, and get the right reply. If you are looking for love, the surprise will be that someone you thought so cold is bursting with warm feelings for you. And when you hear this person talk to an audience about animals, you will reach out.

If you are already secure in a relationship, then this person can become a close friend, who helps you reach your peak of confidence and open a partner's eyes to the real, sensual, you.

LIFE READING

An artistic flair for decorating everyday objects in unusual ways can build into a business very quickly, especially if you team up with someone younger and highly enthusiastic. Soon you will see that the barriers in your working life were partly of your own building.

From today, refuse to accept criticism unless it is deserved. For too long it's been a power tool used by someone who should be close to you. A stamp will soon seal a legal document, and a family concerned by one member's intense behaviour will be reassured.

LUCK READING

Politics, big battles and travel facts can all be prize-finders. Special animal knowledge wins you a place on a team of celebrities.

COSMIC COUNSEL

Say: "I forgive others and let the love flow back to my own life."

AIR QUEEN

air QUEEN

The Queen's gifts to you are sympathy, intuition and the bravery to visit new people and places.

LOVE READING

Never before have you felt so in tune with the thoughts and feelings of those around you – or been more able to revise a relationship. Your mind is crystal-clear, and you can find the words to put pleasure and power back on an even footing.

If new love is your goal, someone with a strong mind, strong features, and links to the jewellery trade, is perfect.

LIFE READING

Your whole life can change dramatically, once you break a long-term habit of always saying no to involving yourself with new people and situations. And a woman who is a perfectionist and has survived personal tragedy should be first on your list. She has a business plan that is tailor-made for you.

Don't let frustration over a cash delay spill over into a personal friendship. You must stand strong when a family is set to divide itself over a legal document. Get independent experts to check it, and refuse to take sides. Cut down on caffeine and give up smoking – this time you'll succeed.

LUCK READING

Number skills and a flair for planning routes and organizing trips can lead to lucky breaks. A travel delay brings a big ticket bonus.

COSMIC COUNSEL

Repeat daily: "I have the personal power to turn my life around."

air KING

The King rules over wise decision-making and a mature, honest approach to living and loving.

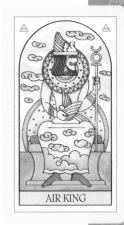

AIR KING

LOVE READING

A relationship will strengthen when both sides can really talk about what they want, without embarrassment or blame. For now, each side has to guess, and gets it wrong too many times. Cut through stubborn pride to win back all that's best in love, and be prepared to suggest some more exciting, unconventional ideas.

New love has a link to an older person with an official role that brings them close to your life. And although at first sight this is someone who seems too tough for you, there's real caring.

LIFE READING

Unhappy feelings are fading out of a work setting but, before you can move on, you need to talk about some difficult subjects, perhaps to a lawyer. The time is coming to tap into your secret skills of presenting people or products in the most effective ways.

You have the will-power, at last, to sort out family cash questions. A child's dream of performing on television, with a famous face, could come true. Tackle life at a slower pace.

LUCK READING

Money, luck and prizes come from hidden names. An official letter frees cash and a removal company could have your name on it.

COSMIC COUNSEL

Say: "I open my heart fully to life and this will attract love to me."

ace of WATER

ACE of WATER

The ace is a fruitful, productive card, promising happiness, rewards and the joy of new birth.

LOVE READING

Even if you are less than happy with the love levels in your life right now, this card promises new riches – if you look in the right place. In an existing relationship, this means going back to simple values of friendship and respect and letting out those passionate ideas you have.

If you are seeking love, then a person who adores mystery stories, on the screen or the page, can be your perfect match.

LIFE READING

Creative projects, especially any linked to design, can get off to a strong start – and there is cash to be gained, too, if you refuse to be rushed. This time, never lose sight of your personal happiness needs.

Something you have been seeking for so long is now there for you, close to your home. A family find once again the security they need, and could increase suddenly – this card is also known as the christening card! A building that resembles a boat helps health.

LUCK READING

New parents, new pastimes and prizes linked to TV questions are all luck-bringers, along with the number 1 and a marked map.

COSMIC COUNSEL

Repeat often: "I welcome new love, new people, into my world."

two of WATER

Couples, double success, and new trust that is both given and taken, are the themes of this card.

TWO of WATER

LOVE READING

A balanced love-bond, with the right mix of mental and physical, can be yours now – but you have to start by giving out the kind of two-way love that you long to receive. Yes, you have been holding back, but from now on you have nothing to fear. The resentment or doubt that has left love one-sided can be faced – and erased. And you can fulfil all those fantasies of pleasure in unusual places.

New romance is linked to a slow, secret smile, and someone who has a role as a "fixer", either professionally or personally.

LIFE READING

Any job in which two people work closely together can lead to cash and the roving lifestyle you prefer – two is also the adventure card. There are strong signs of links to the world of acting, too.

Family bonds that have been over-stretched by difficult situations can mend again – a special shared event is the key. And strong opposition to a house move suddenly slides away. Health is helped by less worry, more laughter, and following a vegetarian diet.

LUCK READING

Pairs of objects, names of wild flowers, light yellow and the number 2 all spell luck – and so does a room that opens on to a garden.

COSMIC COUNSEL

"The power of hope and love can guide my life, if I only let it."

three of WATER

THREE of WATER

Three is a symbol of trust, comfort, healing powers, and getting all sorts of happy endings.

LOVE READING

This is also known as the wedding card, and has the power to bring opposites together, and to turn uncertain relationships into rock-solid matches. But you have a part to play, as this card indicates that it is time for you to take the love lead. You will feel so free, so fulfilled, and ready to share love doubts at first – and then overcome them.

If you seek love, find your dream in a place where a special cake is cut, with someone very different and linked to a healing career.

LIFE READING

Inwardly and outwardly, your home is set to change. A time of strained silence within a family is ending, and new links can be extended, especially to a child from a faraway place. Reach out to help a relative overcome fears, and you too will be rewarded.

An address linked to the sea features in your future. Work-wise, a hidden network of contacts is spreading out, with you at its centre. Yes, you have impressed exactly the right people. Drinking a glass of warm water first thing every morning cleanses your system.

LUCK READING

Cash links you to someone who has been out of your life for three years, a contest in a shop window, and unique jewellery.

COSMIC COUNSEL

Tell yourself: "I value myself and this also helps me value others."

four of WATER

Here's what you'll find in four – fulfilment, and love that takes you towards a better future.

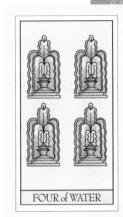

COSMIC COUNSEL

When you've spent so long chasing love, you could feel almost cheated when you catch it. Especially if this is the kind of attraction that centres on looks or status. Scratch the surface and underneath it's empty of real feelings and respect. But given time and space, true love can grow, so don't give up on a relationship – old or new – just yet. The cure lies inside, in honest talking, not outside, in infidelity.

If your heart is still free, meeting someone whose job involves watching over people or places could change that.

LIFE READING

Looking beyond the boundaries of your everyday job (or your search for a job) towards voluntary work could leave you refreshed and full of ideas. And some of them are cash-rich. Any link to consultancy work is lucky, too. Cash comes through on your mother's side, and is split four ways, but with you in control.

Don't ignore the sentimental value of things, or people, in your life. You do need them. If you are the first to reach across a family gulf, others will follow. Beat anger by fast walking.

LUCK READING

Junk-shops, jumble sales and fun bets are among your winners.

COSMIC COUNSEL

Every morning, say this: "I am ready to give, and receive, help."

FIVE of WATER

five of WATER

Five finds you figuring out priorities, pushing dreams forward, and enjoying cash legacies.

LOVE READING

This is the card of clean breaks and clean slates, and shows that you have not really let a past disappointment go. Until you do, the challenges of new or current love will be stifled.

If you are in a relationship, there may be a difficult time when partners' needs don't match, but re-sorting priorities leaves both sides stronger. If you are looking for love, someone who wears theatrical clothes may be right.

LIFE READING

You are entering a time of fast, unexpected change in your working world. If you keep your eyes on the prize, speak your thoughts and share your fears, you will snatch success. See problems in the present as stepping stones to the future. And look closer at careers that are linked to finding lost people or objects.

At home, don't be afraid to give orders – it's what other people want, whatever they say. A missed chance, of a home, a holiday or a baby, comes back. Health changes do best in a group.

LUCK READING

Cooking or growing something, revolving wheels and contests linked to running water are prize-pullers. A gift connected to your birth has special value and the number 41 adds up to luck.

COSMIC COUNSEL

Repeat often: "My greatest gift to myself is forgiveness."

six of WATER

Getting together, growing together – six is a symbol of finding true identity, and new family.

SIX of WATER

LOVE READING

Your passion past is working its way into your present now, as you turn mistakes into experience and emerge more mature and confident. In a relationship, this means being totally honest about problems and tackling them together, rather than looking the other way and waiting for a fairy godmother. Yes, you can give someone freedom – without fear – and find, deep within yourself, a secret sensuality.

If you have not yet found a love to last a lifetime, this could change at an outdoor event linked to selling, where '60s music plays.

LIFE READING

A job or family situation has tested you, but now the rewards are flowing, and at last you can relax. And welcoming a younger person back into your life after a reluctant separation brings a whole new branch of family into your life.

Joining an established team could be the kick-start that a new career needs, especially if it is connected to making people laugh. Exploring your day-dreams releases tension in mind and body.

LUCK READING

What you sell for someone else and how you respond to a sports challenge shapes luck. Six starts a special phone number.

COSMIC COUNSEL

Keep in your heart and mind: "Each day offers new happiness."

SEVEN of WATER

seven of WATER

Psychic seven is a card of choice – fly high to follow a dream, or stay anchored in happiness.

LOVE READING

Someone with pale eyes and a passion for computer games could be such a great partner for you, if you are free right now. And the two of you will meet in a place where most people are reading or writing. Beware of setting love sights too high, however, and refusing to settle for anything but perfect passion. Comparing partners to an ideal dream is not fair and lays a relationship open to outside rivals.

LIFE READING

Starting so many things, finishing so few – does this sound like you? The challenge of the seven is to decide to introduce more discipline and order into your working and personal lives. Set spending limits, and allow more time to see plans through.

At home, trust your own instincts about a move, or other decision. This is the card of clear sight, which helps you to make good, if unusual, choices. Soothe your nerves, boost self-confidence and banish secret fears with cycling and swimming.

LUCK READING

A game of guesswork linked to the sea unlocks a chain of family luck. Teams of seven, picnics and heart shapes are lucky, too.

COSMIC COUNSEL

When in doubt, murmur to yourself: "I have the courage needed to create my own life."

106

eight of WATER

Eight is a turning-point card – open the gate to opportunity, and drop harmful ideas and people.

LOVE READING

You are entering a phase when you will not settle for the love you have, but decide on the love you want – and then go for it. If you are in a relationship, this means showing a stronger, more independent side. If you are looking for new love, it means taking up the challenge of an unconventional partner with a lifestyle very different to yours, but who shares an initial with you. Either way, this card's message is to close your heart to outside pressure.

LIFE READING

All that is new and different attracts you now – focus on doing one thing at a time well, rather than wasting energy. Work linked to the world of luxury cruises could come your way. A meeting in a place floored with black and white tiles seals a home deal.

You know deep down that a family has to face upheaval, and you have the words to talk them round. But do fade out a harmful friendship with silence, not panic. Turn vague health ideas into solid changes, starting with careful control of fat intake.

LUCK READING

Cash comes from velvet-covered surfaces and river bridges. A politician's name and white ships are lucky, too.

COSMIC COUNSEL

Say to yourself: "From today, my life will contain more success."

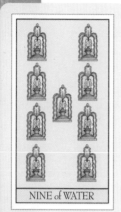

NINE of WATER

nine of WATER

Nine is a signal of sharing, security and strength in the knowledge that the future is truly exciting.

LOVE READING

This wish card slips lovers out of your dreams and into your arms, and releases all the romance that you have been waiting to share. But do be sure that all the passion wishes you make are sincere ones, or they cannot come true.

If you are in a relationship, a slight tension between a couple can disappear in a special night of passion. This reminds both partners that love can be strong again – though not as clinging and possessive as before. If you are still seeking romance, then someone with sun-bleached hair and several unusual pets, or pictures of animals, can be the one.

LIFE READING

Luck and cash are made to share with those around you – anything you give will come back double. Keep sight of your ultimate goal at work, and refuse to let minor set-backs slow you down. Swapping skills or experiences with someone who lives very close could lead to a brilliant career chance.

A home by the sea, and news of a child, send family shadows fleeing. Small changes in eating habits are good health moves.

LUCK READING

Luck-leads are a sentimental trip, number 49 and unsigned cards.

COSMIC COUNSEL

Repeat: "I care for my mind and body and find the love I need."

ten of WATER

Ten tells you to leave your comfy life and reach for a rainbow of success, happiness and love.

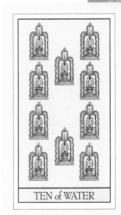

TEN of WATER

LOVE READING

It looks like a relationship that other people disapprove of, or which challenges ideas of conventional happiness, could work so well – this is a strong card that helps you win the hearts you really want. But, both in new love and old, you must be ready for upheaval, as work or family chances take one partner away, at least for a while.

However, this is also the card of long engagements and complicated situations becoming simpler. Your destiny partner often wears stripes and drives a car with a girl's name.

LIFE READING

Beware of exploiting someone else's feelings or finances, either at work or at home. You have more advantages than you realize, and even if things are already going your way, they will get better.

Long-distance work-links reach into your life, and the key is someone you met in your first job, or at school. Responsibilities in a family don't go away, but are lightened by sudden cash help. Get an early night at least once a week, and eat more raw food.

LUCK READING

When a group choose the same number several times it is lucky, and photography contests and the number 28 bring fortune, too.

COSMIC COUNSEL

Say this to yourself: "A stranger is just a friend I haven't met yet."

WATER PRINCESS

water PRINCESS

The Princess rules over illusion and images – so nothing is what it seems, not even yourself.

LOVE READING

However many times you've been in love, you still have so much to learn. If you are in a relationship, realizing that real love can shake under spiteful words or stormy actions, but it will not sink, is lesson number one. Lesson number two is to speak what's in your heart, even if you feel a partner will not like it.

If you are still seeking lasting love, someone who always looks different, even in the most ordinary clothes, is right for you.

LIFE READING

All work that has aspects of illusion would be perfect for you, including cinema, theatre, magic – and taking or making pictures. And, whatever your age and expectations, you could soon find yourself sitting a special test.

In a family, someone who seems very young announces sudden love plans that are a shock. But don't react without all the facts. A building that is not yet finished has a key role to play in your future. Don't let your health be held hostage by moods.

LUCK READING

A train ticket, prizes of jewellery, and a chance to study a very different subject, are all lucky. So are letter-linking games.

COSMIC COUNSEL

Make your motto: "I appreciate myself so I can appreciate others."

water PRINCE

A stimulating mix of fresh ideas, younger lovers and freedom make up the Prince card.

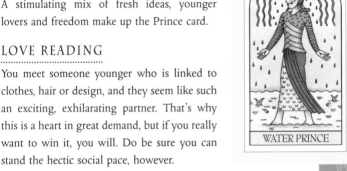

LOVE READING

You meet someone younger who is linked to clothes, hair or design, and they seem like such an exciting, exhilarating partner. That's why this is a heart in great demand, but if you really want to win it, you will. Do be sure you can stand the hectic social pace, however.

If you are in a relationship, then the way to share more love with someone is to see them less. Develop some interests of your own and stop worrying whether a work goal is worth it – it is.

LIFE READING

There is an ideal working world for you linked to selling or sharing other people's creative work. And it starts when you look after an object or a place while someone is away. Positive financial changes follow when cash is returned, and a very quiet, dreamy member of a family has some startling news.

Across your life, there are new directions to choose, but do try to shake off that need for constant approval. You can do things on your own, and do them well. And never miss breakfast!

LUCK READING

Horses lead you to luck, and any firm or uniform that has an animal logo is a fortune-finder. Win with written love words.

COSMIC COUNSEL

Say it and believe it: "Challenges bring out the best in me."

WATER QUEEN

water QUEEN

Understanding, sympathy and intuition all flow from the Queen, with a helping of intrigue, too.

LOVE READING

After some difficult times, you are moving into a period when love can be all you want, all you deserve. Your own feelings, and those of a lover, seem really straightforward. But beware of understanding too well, too completely, and not maintaining the element of mystery that keeps love fresh. Talk through child-related subjects again.

If you are seeking love, then someone with eyes of brightest green, who works in photography or advertising, is the one.

LIFE READING

If your working world is not yet geared to helping others, on whatever level, perhaps it is time to change. For this card shows that you have special gifts for sympathy, practical help, alternative therapies and helping other people share painful memories.

Never have your instincts been so sharp, in all areas of your life. You should, and you must, trust them. A change of neighbours brings glamour. Tension starts with pent-up emotions – let them out.

LUCK READING

A trip or holiday that you help to arrange could end in a prize. An animal rescue society, codes, musical clues and finishing slogans also bring luck.

COSMIC COUNSEL

Breathe deeply and slowly and say: "I am so calm and strong."

water KING

The King is a symbol of support and mature emotions, a calm, clear approach to life, and love.

WATER KING

LOVE READING

Someone with unique physical and emotional love skills, who is very much in demand, comes into your life. What starts as friendship can grow into passion, and both sides find special ways to make it last. Look out for this exciting meeting when you take a child to the cinema.

If you are already in a relationship, you must accept that the intensity and excitement of early passion has to pass, after which it takes more work to keep it alive. Try to relax and let feelings out.

LIFE READING

Negotiations go very well for you, especially when you are offered help from a man who has his own business. You have a secret talent linked to making homes for people who really need them.

A family's future looks bright when someone outside starts trying to trace some lost cash on your behalf. You've stumbled into the sympathy trap with people at home – it's time now to give some tough love so that they can solve a problem for themselves. A gentle scalp massage may help to soothe thoughts.

LUCK READING

A place with a name linked to ships is a fortune-fixer, along with hearing about a contest on an open-air broadcasting system.

COSMIC COUNSEL

Say daily: "When I expect the best results, I will get them."

TAROT IN ACTION – SOME SAMPLE READINGS

PERSONAL THREE-CARD READING

This is a very direct way to do a personal reading. First, a "questioner" card is selected, to represent the person having the reading (see pages 12-13). Then the client shuffles the cards and cuts them into three piles and the reader takes one card from the top of each pile, in turn.

The card taken from the top of the centre pile is CARD ONE
The card taken from the top of the left-hand pile is CARD TWO
The card taken from the top of the right-hand pile is CARD THREE

- CARD ONE reveals what is really on the mind of the person consulting the Tarot.

- CARD TWO reveals what action will deal with this in the immediate future.

- CARD THREE looks at the outcome in the more distant future.

Remember that, when a card is reversed (taken out upside down), this does not give it a negative meaning, but simply weakens its impact a little. Take time to look at the cards. And, yes, you can do readings for yourself, as well as for others.

Please note: all names in the following examples have been changed in order to protect privacy.

LINDA'S READING

When Linda came to see me she was simmering with uncertainty. She had just qualified as a nurse and was about to marry Tom, a surgeon at the same hospital. They were in love, there were plans to have children in a couple of years' time, and everything seemed idyllic – and yet...

The QUESTIONER CARD was the EARTH PRINCESS
This represented Linda, a 24-year-old Virgo.

CARD ONE WAS THE THREE OF EARTH

This can be a strong marriage card, confirming that Linda does have the protective warmth of love in her life. But it also shows that the heat of love alone is not enough to sustain a relationship. It needs a strong framework of friendship, because friends can often talk more honestly about what they want from life than lovers can.

Earth is the element of ambition and it suggests that Linda has been hiding what she really wants to achieve in life – in case it damages love. But this is a dangerous tactic. This card also links with the world of caring, especially caring for children – not just as a mother, but as a health professional.

At this point, Linda interrupted to say that, although she had just qualified as a nurse, she had known for at least a year that what she really wanted was to be a children's doctor. She had not, however, shared this with Tom, in case it damaged their happiness and his plans for their future. It was this unfulfilled ambition, not love and marriage, that was dominating her mind. It was time to turn over the second card.

CARD TWO WAS THE WORLD

This shows that your personal world is widening and that the talent you secretly wish for is there. So Linda is perfectly capable of becoming a doctor. And there is a strong international flavour to this card. The World card also speaks of reaching out to people. And, of course, the first person she had to reach was Tom... she had to reveal her true ambitions to him.

CARD THREE WAS THE EIGHT OF EARTH

This card refers to bringing calm order to the chaos of thoughts and emotions, and the confidence that comes from doing the work that you know is right for you. So Linda will achieve her ambitions. This is also a strong family-centred card and talks of different generations working together and finding enrichment for all of them.

THE OUTCOME

This reading was done for Linda 15 years ago. She did go on to train as a doctor, with her husband Tom's full support. They did have their children, and both sets of grandparents shared in the child care. For several years Linda and Tom worked together in Africa, running a hospital that specialized in mother and baby care.

ANSWERING THE QUESTION

This approach is the most direct way of answering a specific question. First, a questioner card is selected, to represent the client. Then the client shuffles the cards and cuts them into two piles, all the time thinking about the question. He or she then takes one card from the top of each pile and places them face down.

• The card from the top of the left pile is CARD ONE
• The card from the top of the right pile is CARD TWO
Now the client shuffles the cards again until he or she feels ready, and then deals the top card and places it , face down, between the other two. This is CARD THREE

CARD ONE   CARD THREE   CARD TWO

SUE'S READING

Sue was a former model and, at 39, still very beautiful. Her life had been filled with romantic adventures. Now, though, she wanted to marry and have a child. But she was involved with two very different men and was finding it difficult to choose between them. Both had talked about marriage. Sue selected her three Tarot cards and left them, face-down, on the table. As we turned them over, one by one, this is how the Tarot helped her to answer her pressing question.

The QUESTIONER CARD was the AIR QUEEN
Sue is a 39-year-old Libra, so her card is the Air Queen.

CARD ONE WAS THE EARTH KING

This is the card of wealth, signalling a man who has achieved riches and personal power. He controls other people with his sheer determination and appreciates money mainly for the comfort and style it can buy. Sue was already driving a car he had given her, and wearing a Chanel suit he had chosen for her. This card shows Sue a life of luxurious security. He would want his children to be achievers, yet could spoil them by wanting them to have all the things he had worked for. He would be a reliable husband, yet a great deal of his emotion and fulfilment would be involved in his business.

Sue interrupted to say that, yes, this was Jack, a self-made millionaire. He would certainly be a great provider. And, as a bonus, he was sexy and handsome, too. Her friends told her she would be crazy to turn him down, but...

CARD TWO WAS THE ACE OF WATER

This is a mind card. It denotes a restless idealist, someone who cares about the environment and yet has a powerful sexuality and never quite grows up. This helps him to understand children and yet not take full responsibility for supporting them. His career is constantly changing. Sometimes he earns money and then just

118

ACE of WATER

whistles it all away, almost overnight. There is excitement, adventure and discoveries to be made with this person – though the journey would never be in five-star luxury. Oh, yes, said Sue, that's David. He writes music for a living, lives in a cottage close to the sea and is always embarking on some new campaign to save the world.

CARD THREE WAS THE STAR

It is the third card that helps Sue to make her choice. Its image shows

STAR

that she needs to trust her own talents a little more. Although she is drawn to the richer man, because of the responsibility she feels towards the child she wants to have, it's time to think of the things that really enrich life – and admit that she wants some adventure and idealism in her life. In the past, a need to spend money merely hid a spiritual dissatisfaction.

This card makes music a strong love clue. It asks for sincerity and reminds you that those who marry for money may find each penny is hard-earned.

THE OUTCOME

This reading was done three years ago. She is now married to David and is expecting her third child. They live very simply by the sea, and she has discovered her own talent for writing words that go with his music. She has no regrets about Jack, the millionaire, even though she still sees him from time to time – he married her sister, who loves both Jack and the luxury lifestyle he can bring her.

119

THE DESTINY READING

This doesn't solve a dilemma but simply looks into the future with a three-card deal. Once the questioner card is chosen, the client shuffles the cards and cuts them into three piles. The piles are numbered as on page 114, but their meanings are:

2. TURN OVER
CARD TWO

1. TURN OVER
CARD ONE

3. TURN OVER
CARD THREE

- CARD ONE represents life and career.

- CARD TWO represents your love-life.

- CARD THREE represents the outcome of the situation.

JOYCE'S READING

When she came to see me, Joyce explained that nothing was really wrong – but nothing was really right, either. She had said goodbye to a going-nowhere relationship and had outgrown her present job. What could the Tarot tell her? During the reading, Joyce took time to look really deeply at the images on the cards.

The QUESTIONER CARD was the AIR QUEEN
Joyce was a 33-year-old Gemini, making the Air Queen her card.

CARD ONE WAS THE WHEEL OF FORTUNE

This is the strongest sign of dramatic changes. And the challenge is to accept that you need to spin your life in a new direction. It takes courage to accept that you can live and work in a totally different way. That you can leave a job that brings only disappointment into your life, and accept one that has an element of risk, yet feels so right. But you have to act very decisively. A job will not be offered twice.

An opportunity to meet a destiny lover must also be accepted. To win a contest, you must be in it! When luck is not used, it rolls right past you. Within ten days, a work opportunity would be there. There would also be a meeting in a revolving restaurant, and someone whose name started with "W" would be part of it. Constant travel and welcoming new people into her world were also strongly starred with this card.

CARD TWO WAS THE MAGICIAN

Another card from the Major Arcana – yes, Joyce's life is moving fast! The love-partner who can change everything will be providing the

121

entertainment at a party where she is a guest. She must look deeper than his rather loud clothes and wild ways to find real warmth and understanding.

To be sure of meeting this man, she must accept an invitation to a party or other gathering where she will know no one, and wear a crimson dress that she has in her wardrobe yet, so far, has not worn.

"Let me get this straight," Joy interrupted. "First, I have to take this job – if there even is a job – and never stop travelling. And at the same time, I'm going to meet my destiny lover." She shook her head in a rather disbelieving way, yet still lurched forward eagerly as I dealt the third card.

CARD THREE WAS THE CHARIOT

It's very unusual, and very interesting, when all three cards are dealt from the Major Arcana. And it shows that a time of inaction is over. All the opportunities are there, but there is more than one kind of journey to make. You will need to go on an inner journey that takes you far from doubt, from diving away from life, to accepting opportunities and believing that you can steer your life towards luck and love.

THE OUTCOME

A year on from her reading, Joyce wrote to me from a cruise-liner. She had taken up all the opportunities outlined for her on the cards. She had gone to the party, in the revolving restaurant, met her destiny lover, the entertainer, and was now working as his manager on a tour of the world. She was, she said, living out her dreams.

122

THE 12-CARD LIFE SPREAD

This is based on the 12 sectors of the horoscope. It's a good, once-a-year guide that gives a reading for each area of your life.

First, the reader takes the questioner card from the pack – the card that identifies the client. This card is placed in the centre of the circle. The client then shuffles the cards, cuts them and hands them back to the reader. They are dealt, from the top of the pack, like the signs of the zodiac, in an anti-clockwise direction (see diagram below). Each card governs different sectors of the client's life circle, as follows:

- CARD ONE represents the personality sector.
- CARD TWO represents money and personal values.
- CARD THREE represents family and communication.
- CARD FOUR represents home and emotional security.
- CARD FIVE represents prize-winning and creative talents.
- CARD SIX represents work and health.
- CARD SEVEN represents marriage and other partnerships.
- CARD EIGHT represents the deepest emotions.
- CARD NINE represents truth and learning.
- CARD TEN represents ambition and achievement.
- CARD ELEVEN represents friendship and social life.
- CARD TWELVE represents secrets, hopes and fears.

ALAN'S READING

The following 12-card reading was done for Alan, who is 35 and works in the sports world.

The QUESTIONER CARD was the FIRE KING
Alan is an Aries, so his personal card is the Fire King.

CARD ONE WAS THE TEMPERANCE CARD

If you get this card, it means that balance, reason and intelligence all flow through you. Strangers who are confused by your calm, reasonable manner may think that you are weak. They, however, soon learn what your friends and team-mates already know – that you are very strong and determined. Others trust you, and you respect this trust and never betray it.

CARD TWO WAS THE TWO OF EARTH

With this card, there were signs that Alan was over-stretching himself financially, or that a partner was taking too much and giving too little. This could be put right by scheduling time for honest talking. Alan needed to value himself and his talents much more highly. Others take you at your own valuation.

CARD THREE WAS THE THREE OF WATER

This means that someone in the family who has been so difficult to reach, even hostile, is ready to change. Although Alan is not the one to blame, he is the one who needs to make a small apology to get things moving. This is also called the wedding card – and a wedding or anniversary could be where real reconciliation between members of the family will happen.

CARD FOUR WAS THE SIX OF EARTH

This suggests that the move – or total change-around in how a house looks – that Alan wanted for so long can happen now. A house close to a famous forest will play a part in his future. He'll see it for the first time within the next six months, and yet there will be a shock of recognition when he does see it. He could find that it has already played its part in his family history, and this fact inspires him.

CARD FIVE WAS THE FIRE PRINCE

This card signifies that a knowledge of sport and questions asked in front of television cameras can stir prizes. And the way you answer could lead to a new way of earning money.

Your first thoughts are the finest in multi-choice answers. And choosing numbers with the relation or friend who looks most like you will go well.

CARD SIX WAS THE STRENGTH CARD

This is one of the major cards, so Alan should be ready for big changes, like moving from team player to manager. He is going to have the emotional courage and strength needed.

If Alan was not working at this time, then this card would point to a career linked to animals. An excellent health card, it asks you to co-operate by dealing decisively with a situation that rips into your nerves.

CARD SEVEN WAS THE THREE OF AIR

This suggests that a current marriage is strong and satisfying, yet it is important never to assume that you know everything about a partner. If Alan makes a decision to rekindle tenderness with a romantic holiday, he could unleash new loving.

A business partnership will be offered by someone who provokes a mixed reaction. Yet it has great potential.

CARD EIGHT WAS THE WATER KING

Time to show tough love to a family member who needs to be independent. Keeping secrets to protect other people is a dangerous tactic. Slowly share more.

Although you are strong, learning to ask for help when you need it is wise, not weak. Someone with healing hands, who could be a doctor or physiotherapist, will help you make a key choice about life.

CARD NINE WAS THE TOWER

Here, Alan has a major card that turns what at first may look like an unwelcome upheaval into a triumph – as long as the situation is tackled with optimism and determination. Learning a new skill, or perhaps finding a new way of being involved in a job he's always loved, will be absolutely vital. So is adopting a realistic approach to fitness levels.

CARD TEN WAS THE SUN

It is important for anyone getting this card to seize the chance that will be offered, even though it seems to come at a strange time. It suggests that Alan will be helped by a powerful man who controls a large fund of money and has big sporting ambitions. An ambition that leads to a silver cup is going to be achieved. And Alan will reach one achievement by a different route.

CARD ELEVEN WAS THE SEVEN OF FIRE

A group of people who play sport together will be – or will remain – right at the centre of Alan's life. Travelling with them across Europe will bring enormous personal happiness and satisfaction. And Alan should say yes when he is invited to sing on a charity record – he will soon find that this is just the starting point of an amazing adventure.

CARD TWELVE WAS THE SEVEN OF AIR

The second seven in one reading confirms the need for action. Within just seven weeks, life could be very different. But this does mean choosing a direct route, not being tempted by cunning detours or avoiding the facts. Although things are going to happen very quickly, it is important that Alan takes time to calm his mind, then the decisions he makes will be good, and so will his future.

THE OUTCOME

This reading helped Alan to make the change from being a sports player to being a team manager – a recurrent injury that he had been trying to cover up was making it more and more difficult to play. To his surprise (though it was on the Tarot), he enjoyed his new job enormously and found great international success.